H IS FOR HISTORY:

USING CHILDREN'S LITERATURE TO DEVELOP HISTORICAL UNDERSTANDINGS

by Laurel R. Singleton

**Social Science Education Consortium
Boulder, Colorado
1995**

ORDERING INFORMATION

This publication is available from:

Social Science Education Consortium
P.O. Box 21270
Boulder, CO 80308-4270

ISBN 0-89994-385-3

© Copyright 1995 Social Science Education Consortium

CONTENTS

INTRODUCTION

> You want to keep these things in mind: history and family.
> How they are often inseparable. In the twentieth century you
> may feel that all those things that went before have little to do
> with you, that you are made immune to the past by the pre-
> sent day: All those dead people and conflicts and ideas—why,
> they are only stories we tell one another. History and politics
> and conflict and rebellion and family and betrayal. Think
> about it.
>
> *How to Make an American Quilt,*
> by Whitney Otto (New York: Random
> House, 1991).
>
>
> These things he told to his grandsons carefully, slowly and at
> length, because they were old and true, and they could be lost
> forever as easily as one generation is lost to the next, as easily
> as one old man might lose his voice, having spoken not
> enough or not at all.
>
> *House Made of Dawn,* by Scott
> Momaday (New York: Harper & Row,
> 1968).

Children's Literature and History

Works of children's literature can provide "compelling stories that invite students to identify with and care about social studies content" (Sage 1993). Books or stories with historical settings can provide "authentic glimpses of daily life in a past era...As children develop a deep understanding of the lives of others, they can improve their understanding of themselves and their heritage" (Harthern 1993). Such views of the part children's literature can play in social studies education generally and history education specifically are shared by many educators today.

With the growth of the whole language movement, social studies educators have begun reconsidering the role literature might play in developing young people's understanding of history and geography, as well as other aspects of the social world.

McGowan and Guzzetti (1991) suggest several reasons why trade books can enhance social studies instruction:

1. Trade books are more readily comprehensible than textbooks, and they are available to suit a wide range of ability levels. Thus, trade books can increase the likelihood that all students will experience success in social studies.

2. Trade books are of high interest. Their engaging writing style and "sense of direction" make them more enjoyable than textbooks and therefore more likely to be read by students.

3. Trade books help students relate their own experiences to classroom content, a key factor in learning. Textbooks are rarely able to make these kinds of links between concepts and everyday experience.

Zarnowski (1993) also points out that while textbooks provide "brief and simple explanations of complex topics," literary works can be used to provide multiple perspectives and to show the varying interpretations that can be given to a historical event. Because literary works engage students at several levels, Zarnowski also believes they can be a tool for encouraging in-depth exploration of historical topics.

While Downey and Levstik's review of the research on history teaching showed that research to be "thin," the studies they analyzed did indicate that young students can understand time concepts as well as logical relationships among events, including temporal and causal relationships (Downey and Levstik 1991). In addition, the studies reviewed indicated that use of narrative—writing shaped as a story—appears to have positive effects on students' historical understanding. Indeed, one study (Levstik 1989) even indicated that reading and discussion of literary narratives could encourage student's interpretation and analysis of text versions of the same events. Thus, the research available supports the use of literature in teaching young students history.

Cautions in Using Literature in the Social Studies Classroom

This resource book is based on the belief that children's literature and history should be linked in elementary classrooms. The children's books mentioned are only a few of the many that could be used to develop historical understandings; our suggestions for their use are intended to serve as models. While children's literature *can* enhance history instruction, some cautions are in order. As Hepler (1988) has pointed out, activities developed around works of children's literature "should serve the reader and the book first, not some particular curriculum area. When the latter happens, *Charlotte's Web* becomes the basis for a science unit on spiders or a social studies theme of 'farming,' although to a child, the story may be about the power of friendship, or learning to stand up on your own piggy trotters."

Other cautions emerge from Levstik's observations of a class using literature as a vehicle for studying history. Levstik (1986) noted that "literature raises issues in an emotionally charged context." Thus, students need an opportunity to move beyond "their initial emotional response to an examination of the different perspectives involved..." Levstik noted that students tended to accept the historical information presented in literary works as "unimpeachable." In using literary works, teachers should therefore be vigilant about encouraging students to question the accuracy of the information presented.

Selection of appropriate materials is also a concern. In analyzing literary selections used in the K-3 texts of the Houghton Mifflin social studies series, Alleman and Brophy (1994) found some examples of effective uses of literature. They also, however, found examples of selections that focus on "relatively trivial or peripheral" aspects of social studies topics or goals, selections used in ways that trivialized the content (this was especially true when folk tales or myths were used), selections used to promote language arts goals rather than social studies goals, and selections that actually create misconceptions.

These problems highlight the importance of careful selection of literary works. Harthern (1993) suggests three criteria for selecting literary works for use in elementary history classes: the books should (1) have authentic settings, (2) involve realistic characters, and (3) reflect experiences, conflicts, and problem resolutions of the time. Alleman and Brophy (1994) suggest that teachers consider the following questions when selecting literature for use in social studies:

1. Does the source match the social education goals for the lesson and unit?

2. Does the source offer sufficient value as a source for social education content and a basis for social education activities to justify the social studies time that will be allocated for it?

3. Does the work seem to be of appropriate length given the social knowledge that needs to be included for adequate sense-making?

4. Does the work enhance meaning and not trivialize the content?

5. Does the work reflect authenticity and promote understanding of the content?

6. Does the work enrich social studies understandings as well as promote language arts or other subject-matter content or skills?

7. Does the source avoid potential misconceptions, unnecessarily shallow interpretations, or stereotypes in its depiction of people and events?

As most teachers are aware, historical children's literature has recently become more realistic, including the darker side of some events. For example, several recent novels about the mill girls deal with sexual abuse. Consequently, it is critical that teachers read every book before assigning it to ensure that it is suitable for their students and the community. In addition, teachers should select literature to balance the heroic and villainous, the tragic and the triumphant. While even young students do not need an overly rosy view of the past, neither will they benefit from an unremittingly negative view.

A number of sources are available to help teachers with the selection task. Annually, a National Council for the Social Studies committee, with assistance from the Children's Book Council, prepares a list of recommended children's trade books in the social studies; the list appears in the April/May issue of *Social Education*. Many of the books used in this publication were taken from recent years' versions of this list. Another journal of NCSS, *Social Studies and the Young Learner*, carries a regular column on children's literature and social studies. *Booklist*, *The School Library Journal*, *The Horn Book*, and the October issue of *The Reading Teacher* carry reviews of children's literature. These sources and such bibliographies of children's literature as *The Black Experience in Books* (Kirk 1993) and *Through Indian Eyes: The Native Experience in Books for Children* (Slapin and Seale 1992) can make teachers aware of high-quality literature useful in developing historical understanding.

Organization of This Book

This book has three major sections. The first provides a brief overview of eight historical understandings that can be developed using children's literature. These understandings, which were adapted from a list of "history's habits of the mind" in the Bradley Commission report (*Building a History Curriculum* 1988), represent "big ideas" that can help students think meaningfully about historical facts. While students can certainly gain specific historical information from literary works, our goal in advocating the use of literature is to develop students' broader historical perspectives.

The overview of each "big idea" in the first section of the book is accompanied by suggestions for using works of children's literature to develop understanding of that idea. Some specific titles are annotated in conjunction with each idea. While the annotations include grade level suggestions, we recognize that every class includes students with widely varying reading skills. Thus, teachers may want to read annotations for other grade levels, may choose to read books aloud to the class, or may decide to make a range of books available for students to select themselves and then complete projects on. The suggestions for using these specific titles are generally brief. Keeping our first caution above in mind, the suggested activities are not intended to replace enjoyment of the books for their literary merit or their exploration of other important themes. Rather, they are designed to show how historical understandings can be developed through engaging activities that do *not* distract from the books' other merits.

The book's second major section provides guides for using specific works of children's literature to teach historic understandings. These guides are based on a format developed by Hepler (1988). Each guide includes a summary of the book, initiating activities, discussion questions intended to stimulate critical thinking, and follow-up activities. The books included represent a variety of genres and are suitable for a range of grade levels. The guides are also cross-referenced to the historical understandings in the previous section of the book.

The final section of the book presents directions for three thematic history units based on children's literature. The first unit looks at the quilt as a common metaphor in children's literature, examining important aspects of American history represented by the quilt. In the second unit, students explore multiple perspectives on a single event—the Civil War's first Battle of Bull Run—and consider how historians combine these perspectives into a single narrative. In the third unit, students read oral histories from young people involved in the civil rights movement and collect and analyze oral histories of their own.

An index of the books mentioned in the text concludes the book.

Throughout the book, we have tried to provide examples for all grade levels, K-6. We have also drawn on a variety of literary genres, including picture books, realistic fiction, historical fiction, biographies, poetry, and informational books. Most of the books included were published since 1991, but a few are older. We make no claim that the books we have included are the *best* books for use in developing historical understandings. Many other works may be equally or better suited for these purposes. We hope that our suggestions will spark your own ideas for using other works.

References

Alleman, Janet, and Jere Brophy, "Trade-Offs Embedded in the Literary Approach to Early Elementary Social Studies," *Social Studies and the Young Learner* (January/February 1994).

Building a History Curriculum: Guidelines for Teaching History in Schools (Washington, DC: Educational Excellence Network, 1988).

Downey, Matthew T., and Linda S. Levstik, "Teaching and Learning History," in James P. Shaver, *Handbook of Research on Social Studies Teaching and Learning* (New York: Macmillan, 1991).

Harthern, Alvis T., "Using Literature Folders," in Myra Zarnowski and Arlene F. Gallagher, *Children's Literature and Social Studies* (Washington, DC: National Council for the Social Studies, 1993).

Hepler, Susan, "A Guide for the Teacher Guides: Doing It Yourself," *The New Advocate* (Summer 1988).

Kirk, Ersye, *The Black Experience in Books for Children and Young Adults* (Ardmore, OK: Positive Impact, 1993).

Levstik, Linda S., "The Relationship Between Historical Response and Narrative in a Sixth-Grade Classroom," *Theory and Research in Social Education* (Winter 1986).

Levstik, Linda S., "Historical Narrative and the Young Reader," *Theory Into Practice* (1989).

McGowan, Tom, and Barbara Guzzetti, "Promoting Social Studies Understanding Through Literature-Based Instruction, *The Social Studies* (January-February 1991).

Sage, Cherryl, "One Hundred Notable Picture Books in the Field of Social Studies," in Myra Zarnowski and Arlene F. Gallagher, *Children's Literature and Social Studies* (Washington, DC: National Council for the Social Studies, 1993).

Slapin, Beverly, and Doris Seale, *Through Indian Eyes: The Native Experience in Books for Children* (Philadelphia, PA: New Society Publishers, 1992).

Zarnowski, Myra, "Using Literature Sets to Promote Conversation about Social Studies Topics," in Myra Zarnowski and Arlene F. Gallagher, *Children's Literature and Social Studies* (Washington, DC: National Council for the Social Studies, 1993).

USING CHILDREN'S LITERATURE
TO DEVELOP HISTORICAL UNDERSTANDINGS

Our purpose in encouraging you to use children's literature as a vehicle for developing historical understandings is not to have students read works of literature to glean historical "facts." Instead, we recommend that discussion of literary works be focused on developing foundational understandings—"big ideas" that will help students organize and analyze information about specific events, eras, people, and the like. The Bradley Commission refers to these big ideas as "history's habits of mind." The eight understandings we present below are, in fact, adapted from a list of 13 that appear in the commission's *Building a History Curriculum.*

Because of the attention the recently released national history standards have received, it seems prudent to discuss why we did not use them as organizers for this section of the book. First, the standards for grades K-4 and 5-12 are organized differently, making it difficult to organize a K-6 resource, such as this book, in concert with the standards. While the historical understandings we describe below have similarities with the content standards in historical thinking, large portions of the standards documents are devoted to standards related to particular topics (K-4) or periods (5-12). In preparing this book, we were less interested in insuring coverage of specific topics or periods than in illustrating how literature can be used to develop historical perspectives. Thus, the "habits of mind" are more suitable for our purposes than the history standards. Of course, the literary works we annotate below and the instructional strategies we describe throughout the book can also be used in support of the standards.

The following are the historical understandings discussed in this section:

1. Real people experienced past events and issues and made decisions that affected those events.

2. The past is important in our lives and to our culture.

3. Change and continuity are both natural parts of the human story.

4. People throughout history were different from each other but also had many things in common.

5. Individuals have made a difference in history, for both good and ill.

6. Events have multiple, complex causes; some causes may be nonrational and/or accidental.

7. Geography and history are related.

8. We construct our knowledge of the past by asking questions, seeking information from many sources, and sorting, evaluating, and analyzing the information.

We believe that developing students' understanding of these ideas at the elementary level will not only provide a framework into which they can place historical facts but also provide a foundation for more sophisticated historical study at the secondary level. You will notice that we do not include a "big idea" about chronology. This does not mean, however, that we do not value the skill of chronological thinking. Throughout the discussion of the understandings below, we include a number of activities designed to enhance chronological skills.

For each of the "big ideas," we suggest a number of books that can be used to develop student understanding. Of course, many books can be used to develop several understandings, but we have chosen to illustrate each book's relation to a single understanding as a means of helping teachers generate ideas about each "big idea." For each book listed, we suggest grade levels for which it is suited—primary (K-2), intermediate (3-4), and advanced (5-6+). These suggestions are meant as just that; we recognize that the suitability of a book for specific students is best determined by someone who knows well those students, their interests, and their abilities.

1. Real People Experienced Past Events and Issues and Made Decisions that Affected those Events.

Young students may have difficulty imagining that the past could have happened any differently. The sequence of events often seems to be inevitable, the people involved somehow not real individuals. Yet the past, like the present, involved real people who made decisions that affected the outcome of events in which they were involved. As the California *History-Social Science Framework* (1988) describes the process of understanding this aspect of the past, "Historical empathy is much like entering into the world of a drama, suspending one's knowledge of 'the ending' in order to gain a sense of another era and living with the hopes and fears of the people of the time." This is an important idea for young students to grasp. At the same time, students need to begin developing a sense of the context in which events occurred so that they do not judge the actions of people in the past solely by contemporary standards.

Reading historical novels or stories that include well-developed characters in a rich contextual setting is an effective way to develop this understanding. Stories involving children are particularly useful, since young people may be more easily able to place themselves in another child's place. Strategies that can be useful in developing this understanding include conducting post-reading discussions of the factors that caused people in a story to act as they did, asking students to describe the events in the story from the viewpoint of one of the characters, having students draw pictures showing the setting in which the story occurred, and assigning students the task of creating a newspaper or magazine that might have been published during the time the story occurred.

Below are annotated several books that could be used to develop this understanding, arranged from easiest to most difficult to read.

Penny in the Road, by Katharine Wilson Precek, illustrated by Patricia Cullen-Clark (New York: Macmillan, 1989; primary) tells the story of a young boy in 1913 who finds a 1793 penny in the road on his way to school. Throughout the day, he wonders about the boy who might have lost the penny so many years ago, comparing his life with that of the earlier child. At the end of the book, the boy of 1913 is a grandfather, and his children wonder not only about the boy who first lost the penny but about the boy who found it—their grandfather. After reading the book, students could create murals that show similarities and differences in all three time periods—1793, 1913, and the present.

My Prairie Christmas, by Brett Harvey, illustrated by Deborah Kogan Ray (New York: Holiday House, 1990; primary) recounts a family's first Christmas after leaving Maine for the prairie. Central to the story, which is one of several prairie stories by this author, is the father's failure to come home after going out to find a Christmas tree on Christmas Eve. How the family's holiday would have been different in Maine could be discussed, as could their feelings about being away from familiar surroundings and their response to the father's absence. Students could experiment with making some of the homemade gifts, foods, and decorations described in the story and compare these items with ones they might make today, identifying reasons for differences (the family in the story had to rely on things that occurred in nature and could be preserved).

Casey Over There, by Staton Rabin, illustrated by Greg Shed (San Diego: Harcourt Brace, 1994; primary) tells the story of two brothers during World War I. While Aubrey's life continues in New York, Casey is fighting in France. Yet Aubrey, too, takes action, writing to Uncle Sam about his brother. After reading the book, students could identify other ways young people can express themselves about events taking place in the world. Students could also be encouraged to reflect on events currently going on in the world as they go about their everyday activities.

Uncle Jed's Barbershop, by Margaree King Mitchell, illustrated by James Ransome (New York: Simon and Schuster, 1993; primary, intermediate), tells the story of an African-American man in the 1920s and 1930s who dreamed of having his own barbershop. While his dream was delayed by such things as the need to help family members in financial distress and bank failures in the Great Depression, Uncle Jed finally opened his own shop shortly before his death. Teachers could introduce the book by asking students to share their dreams of the future and to speculate about some forces that could make realizing their dreams difficult. The teacher could then point out that both family events and national events can sometimes affect how long it takes people to achieve their goals. After reading the story, the class could discuss the actions that Uncle Jed took to reach his dream, as well as the problems he overcame. Which were family-related? Which had to do with larger events in the nation?

Morning Girl, by Michael Dorris (New York: Hyperion, 1992; intermediate, advanced), describes a Taino family's life before Columbus landed in the Caribbean. The story is told in the alternating voices of 12-year-old Morning Girl and her younger brother, Star Boy. The family faces conflicts, the loss of a baby, and a hurricane, but the family members' love for one another and the island on which they live is obvious. Then, one day during her morning swim, Morning Girl sees a canoe filled with "fat people" who speak a language not known to her. To be polite, she welcomes them ashore. The book ends with an excerpt from Columbus's diary. The author's device of alternating voices could be used to explore different perspectives on the same events. Working in small groups, students could rewrite chapters that are told from Star Boy's perspective to reflect Morning Girl's experience of the same events and vice versa. Students might also consider possible outcomes of the book. What do they think (or know) happened next? Why did Morning Girl welcome the strangers to the island? Would the outcome have been different if she had not done so? Why or why not?

While there is an increasingly rich literature on the lives of African-Americans in slavery, James Berry's *Ajeemah and His Son* (New York: HarperCollins, 1991; intermediate, advanced) provides a unique perspective, describing the lives of Ajeemah and Atu in Africa before being captured by slave traders. The book also chronicles their lives after being sold into slavery in Jamaica. While much about their lives is beyond their control, Ajeemah and Atu do make decisions that affect their fates. After reading and discussing the book, students might construct an illustrated timeline of events in the book, perhaps showing how the lives of father and son diverged in Jamaica by splitting the timeline at the point at which they were sold. Students could also hypothesize about what might have been happening in the lives of loved ones still in Africa.

In *Children of the Fire* (New York: Atheneum, 1991; advanced), Harriet Gillem Robinet presents an incredible, detailed description of Chicago on October 8, 1871—the first night of the great Chicago fire. The story is told from the perspective of an 11-year-old African-American girl named Hallelujah. By tricking her foster parents into letting her go out with their son and then escaping from his care, Hallelujah is able to spend the entire night away from home. Her perceptions of the fire and Chicago itself change as she watches the destruction of the city and interacts with rich and poor from other neighborhoods. To reinforce chronological skills, students might construct a timetable showing Hallelujah's activities on an hour-by-hour basis. They will have to make some inferences about how long various activities took. They may also want to evaluate decisions Hallelujah made throughout the course of the night.

Just Like Martin, by Ossie Davis (New York: Simon and Schuster, 1992; advanced), recounts the story of a young African-American boy who wants to emulate Martin Luther King by participating in the civil rights movement and being nonviolent. The child's father, who served in Korea, feels that nonviolence won't work and his son will be hurt if he participates in demonstrations. As young Stone helps organize church members for the March on Washington, sees a bombing at his church kill two friends, and plans a children's march in honor of the dead children, he watches his father become more and more withdrawn and angry. Finally, the boy decides to hide his father's gun, a decision that has both positive and negative effects. Because the book's events take place in a limited time span in 1963, concluding with President Kennedy's assassination, students could easily research other events occurring during this time period and make a visual display of the events of 1963, showing how the events that impacted Stone fit within a larger context.

While not technically children, the young British soldiers at the center of *War Game*, by Michael Foreman (New York: Arcade, 1993; advanced), are barely beyond adolescence as they head off to the "adventure" of World War I. The book, which will be disturbing to some students, soon makes clear that war is not a game and that the enemy are human, too. The book is illustrated with water colors and such historical documents as army recruiting posters, newspaper clippings, and a Christmas card from the King and Queen. Students who read this book will need time to talk about the view of war that it presents. An appropriate activity to accompany the book would be to have students select one character and write a journal or series of letters from his perspective.

2. The Past is Important in Our Lives and to Our Culture.

This theme relates to the power of history in our lives. Shared stories—whether shared within families, ethnic groups, communities, or even larger groups—help define who we are and what we believe in. They provide a sense of where the individual belongs, in time and place. These stories help us understand "the ideas that have molded us and the ideals that have mattered to us," functioning as a "civic glue" (Cheney 1987).

Shared stories also provide models of how people conduct themselves in private and public life, with "virtue, courage, and wisdom—and their opposites" (*Building a History Curriculum*, 1988). Connecting with a character from historical literature can give young people a sense that they are part of our country's past, as well as its present. Myra Cohn Livingston's poem "This Book Is Mine," published in her collection *I Never Told and Other Poems* (New York: McElderry Books, 1992; all levels) beautifully conveys this idea and would be an excellent way to introduce students to the study of history and historical literature, as would Langston Hughes's poem "To You" and "History of My People," by Walter Dean Myers, both of which are reproduced in the new collection *Soul Looks Back in Wonder*, selected and illustrated by Tom Feelings (New York: Dial Books, 1993; all levels). Yet another poem appropriate for this purpose is "I Ask My Mother to Sing," by Li-Young Lee, reprinted in *Celebrate America in Poetry and Art*, edited by Nora Panzer (New York: Hyperion Books, 1994; all levels).

In developing students' understanding of the importance of history, it can again be a good idea to start with the personal—the importance of family stories—and gradually move out to stories of the larger community. A number of books that can be used to develop this understanding are described below, starting with the easiest to read and progressing to more difficult books:

In *Aunt Flossie's Hats (and Crab Cakes Later)*, by Elizabeth Fitzgerald Howard, illustrated by James Ransome (New York: Clarion Books, 1991; primary), two African-American cousins hear the stories associated with their great-great-aunt's many hats. The stories often link to historic events in the community, such as the great fire in Baltimore or the end of the Great War; other stories relate to purely personal experiences, such as the time Aunt Flossie's hat fell in the water. To the girls, the stories are a perfect prelude to their favorite family meal—crab cakes. The book would provide a good introduction to examining historical artifacts (such as Aunt Flossie's hats) and writing stories that involve the artifacts.

A similar story is told in *May'naise Sandwiches and Sunshine Tea*, by Sandra Belton, illustrated by Gail Fordon Carter (New York: Four Winds Press, 1994; primary, intermediate). The main character in this book enjoys spending afternoons looking through photo albums with her grandmother. Of course, the photos cannot be viewed without family stories being told, too.

A third book revolving around family stories is *The Chalk Doll*, by Charlotte Pomerantz, illustrated by Frane Lessac (New York: Lippincott, 1989; primary). The child in this story is sick; as she gets ready to take a nap, her mother tells her stories from the mother's childhood in Jamaica. The intimate dialogue makes clear that some of the stories have been told many times before. The mother and daughter compare their experiences, building both family and cultural connections. Both this book and the previous two could be used to stimulate student interest in collecting stories from their own family members.

In *The Storyteller*, by Joan Weisman, illustrated by David P. Bradley (New York: Rizzoli, 1993; primary, intermediate), a young Native American girl finds herself in the city far from her home in Cochiti Pueblo, missing her friends and especially her story-telling grandfather. As she strikes up a friendship with an elderly Anglo woman, she learns that sharing stories with friends of many ages and backgrounds creates a new and caring community in the city. A note concluding the book explains the significance of the Pueblo storyteller doll in the story. Students could be encouraged to create a doll of their own design to serve a similar function in your classroom.

Grandmother Five Baskets, by Lisa Larrabee, illustrated by Lori Sawyer (Tucson, AZ: Harbinger House, 1993; intermediate), is the story of a young Creek Indian girl in the 1970s who sets out to learn the lessons of basketmaking and life from an older family member. This experience, shared by many of the young women in the tribe, not only provides a way of passing on knowledge that the elders have gained but of encouraging young people to reflect on their goals. While the story tells of the tribe's annual Pow-Wow, a way of keeping tribal history alive, the heroine of the story also takes part in many activities common across ethnic groups—hanging out with friends, playing ball, sharing dreams for the future, getting ready for school, and the like. Since the girl in the story grew up when many students' parents were young, students might share the story with their parents and ask whether they learned about their family's or community's history, crafts, and other knowledge from anyone like Grandmother Five Baskets. If so, what did they learn and how? If not, why do they think this was true?

In *Have a Happy...* (New York: Lothrop, Lee and Shepard, 1989; intermediate), Mildred Pitts Walter blends the story of a family's financial struggles with an introduction to Kwanzaa, the African-American celebration created to link past and present. Chris, the story's main character, finds strength and courage through the celebration, despite his fears about moving, his father's difficulty finding a job, and his own desires (e.g., for a bike to deliver papers). In conjunction with reading the book, you might share with students the history of Kwanzaa, which was created in 1966 by an African-American professor named Maulana Karenga, who wanted a celebration of values important to black Americans. The Kwanzaa principles described in the story are often paired with African proverbs, which students could illustrate in murals or posters. Students could create artwork showing how the principle or proverb was relevant to Chris's life, African-American life throughout U.S. history, and their own lives. The proverbs are:

- Umoja (unity): When spider webs join together, they can tie up a lion.

- Kajichagulia (self-determination): No matter how full the river, it still wants to grow.

- Ujima (collective work and responsibility): When two elephants fight, only the grass will suffer.

- Ujamaa (cooperative economics): A brother is like one's shoulder.

- Nia (purpose): He who learns, teaches.

- Kuumba (creativity): A tall tree is the pride of the forest.

- Imani (faith): He who cannot dance says the drum is all bad.

Jane Yolen's *The Devil's Arithmetic* (New York: Viking Penguin, 1988; advanced) begins with the main character, fifth-grader Hannah, telling her mother, "I'm tired of remembering." Throughout what to Hannah is an endless Seder, she listens to her grandfather droning on and wishes she were at her friend's house. Then, suddenly, she is transported to Poland, becoming the family friend for whom she was named. As she experiences the horrors of the concentration camps, she wonders if she will ever return to her life in New Rochelle, New York. When she "reawakens" at home, she understands why it is important to remember the experiences of her family and others who shared those experiences. In an author's note, Yolen describes fiction as one way of bearing witness to history, of keeping memory alive. After reading and discussing the story, students might consider other ways, in addition to fiction, of keeping our memories of people and events alive. One such way is through creation of memorials. What kind of memorial would students build to the Jews and others who died in the Holocaust? What kind of memorial would be suitable for events in their own family histories?

Rising Voices: Writings of Young Native Americans, selected by Arlene B. Hirschfelder and Beverly R. Singer (New York: Scribner's, 1992; advanced), presents poetry and essays on a number of topics, including identity. Several of the young writers reflect on the importance of their family/ethnic history in forging their own identities. After reading poems such as "As I Walk Along the Hillside," by Misty Stands in Timber, and "Under One Sun," by Neal Beaumont, students could be encouraged to reflect on and write about their own links with family/ethnic history.

3. Change and Continuity Are Both Natural Parts of the Human Story.

Change is a major concept in history. Indeed, much of what is taught in history classes deals with what, how, and why change occurred. Yet students should also understand that there is continuity in the story of humankind as well. As the authors of the *California History-Social Science Framework* (1988) have written, "...students should understand the sources of continuity....What ideas, traditions, and values explain the absence of change? What combination of ideas and events explains the emergence of new patterns?"

Comparing and contrasting their own lives with those of children in historical stories is an effective way for students to begin realizing that both change and continuity are themes in history. For example, young students could read *Here Comes the Mystery Man*, by Scott Russell Sanders, illustrated by Helen Cogancherry (New York: Bradbury Press, 1993; primary, intermediate), which tells about a peddler's visit to an Indiana family in the early 1800s. Students would find similarities in the children's excitement about new possessions (particularly new technologies) and having a visitor, but would see that both the products the young people wanted and how they obtained them are very different from the possessions today's students have and how they acquire those possessions. Many of the books listed for the first understanding above could be used to help students make similar comparisons.

The National Center for History in the Schools suggests that there are five spheres of activity that students should learn about: the social sphere, the scientific/technological sphere, the economic sphere, the religious/philosophical/cultural sphere, and the political sphere (*Lessons from History* 1992). In developing older students' understanding of continuity and change, teachers may find it helpful to use these spheres to organize discussion; for example, in looking at how the life of a young person in a book is different from their own lives, students could list similarities and differences in each sphere. Students could create a web, using a format like that shown on the next page, which reflects a comparison based on the book *Grasshopper Summer*, by Ann Turner (New York: Macmillan, 1989; advanced). This book tells the story of a family that moved from Kentucky to Dakota Territory following the Civil War, experiencing physical, financial, and psychological hardships. While many of the specific events that happened to them would not happen today, feelings that people—both young and old—have about moving remain very much the same, thus highlighting some of the human values and feelings that provide continuity in the face of change.

Another interesting way to begin focusing students on change and continuity would be using the "book in a bag" technique. On the outside of a paper bag, write the title of the book students will be reading. Inside the bag, place several objects (or pictures of objects) that play a role in the story. For example, for the book *Chicken Sunday*, written and illustrated by Patricia Polacco (New York: Philomel Books, 1992; primary, intermediate), you might place the following items in the bag: an egg decorated in the traditional Ukrainian style, a metal Band-Aid box containing coins, a picture of a hat or hat box, a hymnal, and a piece of fried chicken. Let students examine the objects and identify which are still found today and which are not. Based on the title of the book and the objects, encourage students to speculate on what the book is about. After students have read the book, which tells the story of a Ukrainian-American girl and two African-American boys who want to buy the boys' aunt a new hat for Easter, discuss how life in the book is similar to and different from life today. Also discuss whether any of the students' predictions about the book were accurate.

Some specific titles that would work well to develop this theme are described briefly below, arranged from easiest to most difficult in terms of reading and conceptual level.

Since 1920, written and illustrated by Alexandra Wallner (New York: Doubleday, 1992; primary), recounts 70 years in the history of a neighborhood—from farm to town to run-down city to fire-gutted slum to rebuilt neighborhood. Through the illustrations, students can trace the things that change and those that stay the same. You might follow reading of the book with a walk around the school neighborhood, analyzing what about the neighborhood has probably stayed the same over the past 70, 50, or 20 years and what has changed. What changes have students seen since they started attending your school? What changes do they think will happen in the future?

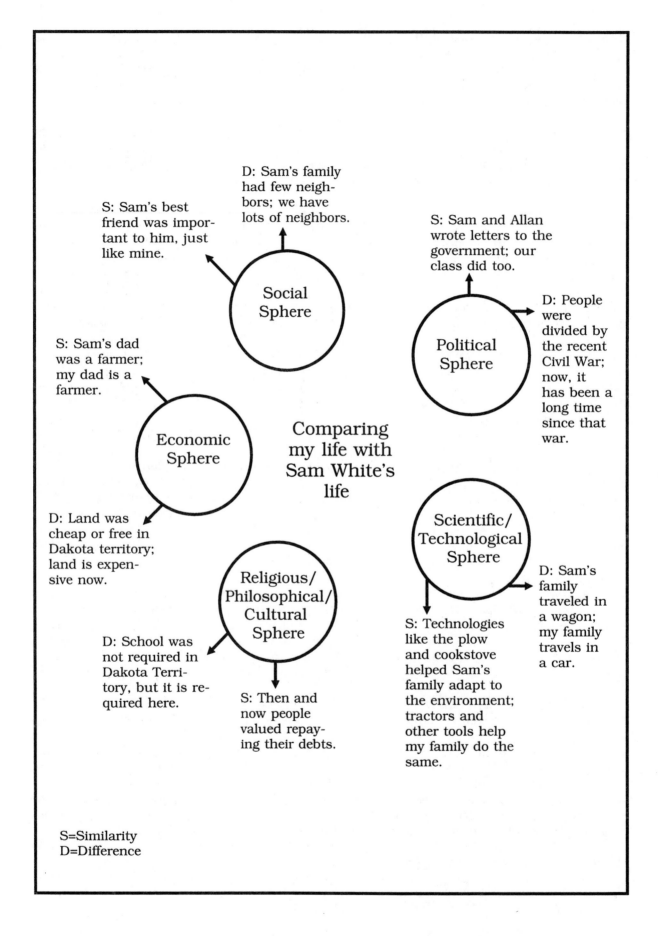

D: Sam's family had few neighbors; we have lots of neighbors.

S: Sam's best friend was important to him, just like mine.

S: Sam and Allan wrote letters to the government; our class did too.

Social Sphere

Political Sphere

D: People were divided by the recent Civil War; now, it has been a long time since that war.

S: Sam's dad was a farmer; my dad is a farmer.

Economic Sphere

Comparing my life with Sam White's life

D: Land was cheap or free in Dakota territory; land is expensive now.

Scientific/ Technological Sphere

Religious/ Philosophical/ Cultural Sphere

D: Sam's family traveled in a wagon; my family travels in a car.

D: School was not required in Dakota Territory, but it is required here.

S: Technologies like the plow and cookstove helped Sam's family adapt to the environment; tractors and other tools help my family do the same.

S: Then and now people valued repaying their debts.

S=Similarity
D=Difference

Continuity and change are explicit themes of *The Always Prayer Shawl*, by Sheldon Oberman, illustrated by Ted Lewin (Honesdale, PA: Boyds Mill Press, 1994; primary). When Adam, a Russian Jewish boy, emigrates, his grandfather stays behind. His grandfather's prayer shawl—totally reconstructed over the years—and his faith remain constants in a world that changes drastically over his lifetime.

In *I Go With My Family to Grandma's*, by Riki Levinson, illustrated by Diane Goode (New York: Dutton, 1986; primary), family members in turn-of-the-century New York travel to Grandma's using several modes of transportation. Students could compare the modes of transportation with contemporary ways of getting from place to place and could consider how the regular family get-together may have changed or stayed the same over time.

A similar exercise could be conducted with students who have read *Great-Grandma Tells of Threshing Day*, by Verda Cross, illustrated by Gail Owens (Morton Grove, IL: Albert Whitman, 1992; primary, intermediate). Students can compare the farm described in the book with a contemporary farm, looking at how the work to be done, the methods used to do the work, and who does the work are similar and different in the two time periods. For urban or suburban youngsters, even making this comparison may require some additional research on contemporary farms. A book that could be useful in this process is *The American Family Farm: A Photo Essay*, with text by Joan Anderson and photos by George Ancona (San Diego: Harcourt Brace Jovanovich, 1989).

Bringing the Farmhouse Home, by Gloria Whelan, illustrated by Jada Rowland (New York: Simon and Schuster, 1992; primary, intermediate), is told from the viewpoint of a little girl whose grandparents have died. The extended family gathers at the farmhouse to divide the grandparents' belongings, providing continuity in the face of a significant change in the family. After students have read and discussed the story, they might talk to their own family members about whether they have items that have passed down from one generation to another. The class could construct their own patchwork quilt, with each student making a construction paper square showing something that represents a family tradition.

Up in the Mountains and Other Poems of Long Ago, by Claudia Lewis, illustrated by Joel Fontaine (New York: Harper Collins, 1991; intermediate, advanced), presents poems describing a young girl's family life in Oregon in the early 1900s. While many aspects of the girl's life are similar to life today (for example, stealing her brother's Easter candy and feeling guilty about making fun of a new girl at school may well be experiences today's students share with the author), other things she experienced would probably not happen today. For example, would the school principal walk the halls with a paddle up his/her sleeve? Why not? A discussion of reasons for similarities and differences might be followed by a writing exercise in which students predict the aspects of their lives that would be similar to and different from a child's life in the middle of the 21st century.

By presenting short stories of growing up in Jerusalem at various times in the 20th century (1910, 1912, 1948, 1950, and 1954), Adele Geras's *Golden Windows and Other Stories of Jerusalem* (New York: Harper Collins, 1993; advanced) provides an excellent vehicle for analyzing continuity and change in one historic setting. Students could create a chart or other graphic showing similarities and differences in the lives of the children in the stories. Which things are enduring? (The importance of family and friends, religious affiliations, etc.) Which change? (How children spend their time, specific events that influence the way children live, etc.) What if the book contained a story set in the present—what might still be the same? What might be a totally new element of the story?

The Star Fisher, by Laurence Yep (New York: Morrow, 1991; advanced), tells the story of an Asian-American girl facing prejudice in 1927 West Virginia. The girl finds strength in two friendships: one with another "outcast" (a girl whose family members are circus performers) and the second with an elderly neighbor. The struggle to "belong" in mainstream society and in the family is a conflict that should resonate with many young people today. An effective comparison could be made with *Maizon at Blue Hill*, by Jacqueline Woodson (New York: Delacorte, 1992), which tells of a similar struggle experienced by an African-American girl at a boarding school where most of the students are white.

4. People Throughout History Were Different from Each Other but Also Had Many Things in Common.

This theme is distinguished from the previous one because it focuses on the diversity that exists within and among locations at any given point in time. No one can deny the rich diversity of cultures and life ways in world history, but with respect to U.S. history, we sometimes think of diversity as a relatively new phenomenon. While the population of the United States is certainly becoming more diverse than ever, the U.S. populace has always been varied. Distinct differences can be seen when, for example, we compare the ways of living and life experiences of urban and rural residents, Hassidic Jews and New England Episcopalians, Scandinavian Americans in Minnesota and the Navajo people of New Mexico. Peoples in widely diverse cultures around the world and across the United States have shown creativity in such areas as the arts and the development of technology and have devised ways of getting along together in communities. They have also faced problems, sometimes solving them successfully, other times with disastrous results. Young people cannot truly understand history if they do not recognize and understand the stories of diverse groups.

At the same time, however, students need to understand that people with different life ways share many things in common. Certain "cultural universals" are found in nearly all human societies—material culture (food, clothing, housing and shelter, etc.); the arts; play and recreation; language and nonverbal communication; social organization, including families and kinship systems; systems of social control; conflict and warfare; economic organization; education; and a world view (belief systems and religion). In addition, U.S. society is predicated on shared commitment to certain democratic values—equality, liberty, truth, rule of law, and the like.

Literature provides an excellent vehicle for exploring not only diversity but also shared experiences and values. Simply providing students with opportunities to read about and compare many cultures and their historical development is one way to approach this understanding. Some specific books useful in developing this theme are:

A Country Far Away, by Philippe Dupasquier (New York: Orchard Books, 1989; primary) presents a single narrative of events in a young boy's life. The dual illustrations—one set of a boy in an African village, the other of a boy in a British or American city—show that people in diverse settings have different ways of living but also share many common aspects of culture, from celebrating the birth of a family member, to playing soccer, to reading books and wishing to make friends with someone in another country. Students who have completed study of a particular time period might create a similar story, showing the lives of young people in two different places during the same time period.

Sitti's Secret, by Naomi Shiab Nye, illustrated by Nancy Carpenter (New York: Four Winds Press, 1994; primary) is a charming story of an Arab-American girl named Mona who visits her relatives in the Middle East. Although she does not speak Arabic and her grandmother (Sitti) does not speak English, they learn to communicate through sign language and the universals of food, play, and touch. When Mona returns to her home in the United States, she writes a letter to the president, telling him "If the people of the United States could meet Sitti, they'd like her too." Mona's experiences and the conclusions she draws about the connectedness of people around the world could provide an interesting basis for a student discussion. Students could draft their own letters to the editor or to a public official describing how they think people around the world are different but connected.

Mrs. Katz and Tush, by Patricia Polacco (New York: Bantam, 1992; primary, intermediate) tells the story of a growing friendship between an elderly Polish-American immigrant and a young African-American boy. Mrs. Katz's stories help Larnel understand the experiences shared by blacks and Jews, including both suffering and triumph. The book is a moving tribute to the power of friendship and could stimulate a provocative discussion of students' own friendships. Do students prefer to be friends with people they perceive as being like themselves? Why or why not? Have they ever found that they have more in common with someone than they originally thought? What rewards do they get from being friends with someone who has had different experiences? similar experiences?

A similar comparison between Polish Jews and African Americans is made in several poems in *All the Colors of the Race*, by Arnold Adoff, illustrated by John Steptoe (New York: Lothrop, Lee and Shepard, 1982; all ages). The poems are written from the viewpoint of a girl whose father is white and mother is black. Her reflections on her own identity and family history are thought-provoking and would provide an interesting complement to *Mrs. Katz and Tush*.

Immigration is an experience shared by the families of most Americans. While the experiences of various groups and individuals varied, the fear of being seen as "different" or strange was shared by many immigrant children. Young Molly of *Molly's Pilgrim*, by Barbara Cohen, illustrated by Michael J. Derancy (New York: Bantam Doubleday Dell, 1983; primary, intermediate), suffers the taunts of her classmates because of how she looks and talks. At Thanksgiving, when Molly's mother makes a Pilgrim doll that looks like a Russian Jew instead of a New England Puritan, even her teacher is puzzled until Molly explains that her mother is also a pilgrim who came to America to find religious freedom, just as the Puritans did. After discussing both the diversity and commonality reflected in this story, students could create their own dolls or drawings showing the immigrants of many nationalities who came to the United States seeking religious freedom.

Mary Downing Hahn's *Stepping on the Cracks* (New York: Clarion Books, 1991; advanced) deals with two types of diversity that may not be examined in children's literature as often as ethnic and religious diversity are—socioeconomic class and diversity of beliefs. The story is set during World War II and deals with the experiences of two middle class girls, Margaret and Elizabeth, and their adversary, Gordy, a boy whom they come to understand better when they discover that he is dealing with problems at home, including economic problems and an abusive alcoholic father. When the girls find out that the boy is sheltering his older brother, who deserted from the army because he believes killing is wrong, they decide to help, despite the fact that their own brothers are serving in the armed forces. Margaret's mother, whose son is killed, cannot forgive the young deserter, however, even after he comes out of hiding to help his family end the abuse, something Margaret's mother was unable or unwilling to do. The book provides rich material for discussion, both of this theme and of change/continuity and the complexity of causes acting on people. Teachers should be careful that students do not take away the idea that abuse is a problem only for people at the lower economic levels.

A Gathering of Pearls, by Sook Nyrel Choi (Boston: Houghton Mifflin, 1994), is the third in the author's series of books about Sookan Bok, a young Korean girl. In this book, set in 1954, Sookan has traveled from Seoul to upstate New York to attend college. Her experiences highlight the differences between Korean and American culture in the 1950s. Yet the importance of family, the power of friendship, and the value of hard work and learning are common to both Sookan and her American classmates. After reading and discussing the book, students could create collections of realia or art works that illustrate the Korean and American aspects of Sookan's life and their common elements.

While set in the present, *Pacific Crossing*, by Gary Soto (San Diego: Harcourt Brace, 1992; advanced), still provides insight into how similar and different histories contribute to similarities and differences across cultures. Lincoln Mendoza, the main character, is a Mexican-American student chosen to spend the summer in Japan. As he learns more about Japanese culture and shares his own culture with his Japanese host family, he learns to more fully appreciate both ways of living. After reading this book, students could write an exchange of letters between Lincoln and his Japanese "brother" Mitsuo or could plan a trip to California by Mitsuo and his family. Where would Lincoln take them so that they could better understand what it means for him to be both Mexican and American?

William Bennett's *The Book of Virtues for Young People* (Parsippany, NJ: Silver Burdett Press, 1996; advanced) could provide an interesting stimulant for student analysis of shared values. Bennett has selected literary excerpts from many cultures and organized them around ten "virtues"—self-discipline, compassion, responsibility, friendship, work, courage, perseverance, honesty, loyalty, and faith. For example, the section on courage includes "An Appeal from the Alamo," a retelling of one of the *Canterbury Tales*, the story of David and Goliath, an excerpt from Anne Frank's diary, an African folk tale, the Greek myth of the Minotaur, and stories about Dolley Madison, Rosa Parks, and Susan B. Anthony, as well as several poems. Students could read the various selections and analyze what each tells us about the value of courage. Students could be encouraged to select or write other stories or poems that could be included in each section of the book. Their selections should reflect how people in diverse cultures and at different times illustrate their commitment to the particular virtue.

A marvelous collection that teachers can use with students at all levels is *From Sea to Shining Sea: A Treasury of American Folklore and Folk Songs*, compiled by Amy L. Cohn, illustrated by 15 Caldecott Medal or Honor Book artists (New York: Scholastic, 1993; all levels). Through folktales, songs, poems, myths, and other stories, the book illustrates the diverse experiences of a wide range of groups who have settled in the United States. For example, a section on the railroad looks at the experience of Irish and Chinese laborers, Native Americans on the plains, and railroad engineers. Yet, the materials also reflect many commonalities: for example, such shared values as hard work, courage, and fun and the importance of beliefs that sustain people in hard times. Another collection useful in the same way is *Celebrate America in Poetry and Art*, edited by Nora Panzer (New York: Hyperion Books, 1994; all levels), which contains poems and artwork reflecting diverse experiences as well as shared values.

5. Individuals Have Made a Difference in History, for Both Good and Ill.

While history is certainly more than the study of "great men," students can benefit from learning about the efforts of men and women who changed the world they lived in. Through studying such people, students learn about the traits and circumstances that contribute to a person's ability to influence events, as well as the ideals and beliefs that motivate influential individuals. As suggested earlier, learning about people of the past can provide models for students to refer to in making decisions in their own lives.

Biographies, autobiographies, and memoirs can be especially useful in developing this understanding. As the Bradley Commission report (1988) stresses, "Biography in particular reveals the significance of individual lives, both of leaders and of ordinary people, as a way of making historical processes and their human consequences real to students."

An interesting way to introduce biographies is to select several people from an era (e.g., the Revolutionary Period) or related to a topic (e.g., women's rights) about whom children's biographies are available. For each person, make a simple wire-hanger mobile. Include provocative quotes from the person, a picture of the person, a map cutout of the state in which he/she was born, items associated with the person (e.g., a kite or bifocals for Benjamin Franklin), and other such materials; do not include anything that shows the person's name. If possible, do not mention the mobiles until students have inspected and asked about them. Let students speculate on the person represented by each mobile. Introduce the biographies available for student reading by matching them with the appropriate mobiles.

Another strategy for use with biographies is to introduce the book by giving a brief description of the subject. Before students read the book, have them write questions about the subject they would like to have answered. They should look for answers to these questions as they read. After they have read the book, they should develop a second list of questions; these should be framed as interview questions they would ask if given an opportunity to talk to the subject. Some questions should ask for additional information about the subject's life, while others should elicit opinions and feelings. If several students have read biographies of the same person, you may have them conduct mock interviews, answering questions as they think the subject might.

Creating "Jackdaws" for the subject of a biography is another useful activity. A Jackdaw is a box containing artifacts and documents that represent the person and the culture in which he/she lived. The items should be selected so that other students examining them will gain a sense of the person's life and times. The box can also be used as a prop if students are asked to present talks as the individuals they have studied. Items in the box will take the place of notecards for the students' presentations.

How individuals make a difference can be stressed through a variety of post-reading activities. For example, each student could create an award to give the subject of a biography read. The award should reflect how the person made a difference in history. Once the award has been created, the student should write a speech he or she might give in nominating the person for the award.

Ask students to identify the most important achievement of the person they are studying. Encourage them to write stories describing how the world today might be different if the person had not been alive to make that achievement.

If students are reading biographies of people associated with a particular topic or issue (e.g., voting rights, the Nobel Peace Prize, technology), a talking timeline can be used to create a cumulative picture of the effects of individual efforts. Each student should read a biography or other material on his/her person and create a brief (no more than one-minute) speech on his/her accomplishments. The speeches should be written in the first person. The following is an example for a talking timeline on winners of the Nobel Peace Prize:

> I am the winner of the 1945 Nobel Peace Prize, Cordell Hull. I was secretary of state for 12 years. Franklin Roosevelt, whom I served under, called me the "father of the United Nations." It was for my efforts in starting the UN, as well as my work to promote peace, that I received the award. I was too ill to accept the award in person, but my written message of acceptance said, "I am firmly convinced that, with all its imperfections, the United Nations Organiza-

tion offers the peaceloving nations of the world a fully workable mechanism which will give them peace, if they want peace."

Students should arrange themselves in chronological order and then present their speeches, creating a talking timeline related to the topic.

Students can make a wide variety of art projects reflecting what they learned about the subjects of biographies. These might include posters, collages, mobiles, and murals. A less familiar medium is the picture cube. A picture cube is constructed of six square sheets of paper taped together in the shape of a cube. Students illustrate or write on five of the sheets before they tape their cubes together. The top sheet is left blank so that string can be attached there to hang the cube. The five sheets should carry:

- A picture of the person selected.

- The person's name and basic biographical information.

- A picture illustrating how he or she made a difference in history.

- One or more quotations from the person.

- A picture of the student's choice.

Completed cubes will resemble the one shown below.

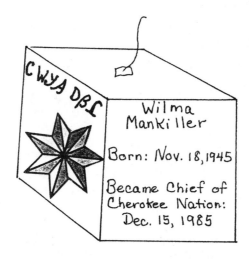

Based on *Wilma Mankiller*, by Caroline Lazo (New York: Dillon Press, 1994; intermediate).

Reading on the idea of how individuals make a difference could be focused on a particular theme, such as working to save the environment. Students could read about well-known people in books such as *Four Against the Odds: The Struggle to Save Our Environment*, by Stephen Krensky (New York: Scholastic, 1993; advanced), which profiles John Muir, Rachel Carson, Lois Gibbs (Love Canal), and Chico Mendes (Amazon rainforest). Other collections that students might enjoy focus on people of particular ethnic groups, such as *One More River to Cross: The Stories of Twelve Black Americans*, by Jim Haskins (New York: Scholastic, 1992; advanced), a book that highlights achievements of African Americans working in a wide variety of fields.

It is also important to acknowledge that individuals do not have to change national or international events in order to make a difference. Doing one's best in the community or school or on behalf of one's friends or family illustrates this idea just as well as actions that benefit the nation or world. The following books provide a look at everyday heroes at various time periods:

Amazing Grace, by Mary Hoffman, illustrated by Caroline Binch (New York: Dial, 1991; primary) is the story of a girl who refuses to accept that she cannot play Peter Pan in the school play simply because she is black and a girl. With the encouragement of her grand-mother and mother, she proves that her acting ability makes her the perfect Peter Pan.

My Great-Aunt Arizona, by Gloria Houston, illustrated by Susan Condie Lamb (New York: HarperCollins, 1992; primary, intermediate), is the charming story of a turn-of-the-century girl who loves to learn and grows up to be an elementary school teacher. Mrs. Hughes taught for 57 years, inspiring and encouraging students, including the author.

The title character of *Sato and the Elephant*, by Juanita Havill, illustrated by Jean and Mou-Sien Tseng (New York: Lothrop, Lee and Shepard Books, 1993; primary, intermediate) is a Japanese artist—a carver of ivory. One day, he discovers a bullet embedded in the piece of ivory he is carving. Suddenly, he realizes that an elephant died to provide the material he carves. He decides to become a stone carver instead.

Pink and Say, written and illustrated by Patricia Polacco (New York: Philomel Books, 1994; intermediate) recounts a Civil War story passed down from generation to generation in Polacco's family. Fifteen-year-old Sheldon "Say" Curtis is wounded in battle and lies uncon-scious for two days until he is rescued by another young soldier, former slave Pinkus "Pink" Ayles. Pink, with his mother's help, nurses Say back to health but is later executed at Andersonville.

The Barn, by Avi (New York: Orchard Books, 1994; intermediate, advanced) is set in 1855 in Oregon Territory. When young Ben is called away from boarding school because his father is ill, he realizes that his older brother and sister believe their father will never recover. Ben convinces them that if the three of them build the barn their father dreamt of, the barn will make him well. While they are ultimately disappointed in their hopes, the three children show great courage and resourcefulness.

Checking on the Moon, by Jenny Davis (New York: Orchard Books, 1991; advanced), recounts the events of one summer in the life of Cab Jones. Cab and her older brother Bill have been sent to stay with their grandmother near Pittsburgh while their mother tours Europe with her new husband, a concert pianist. Crime on the street becomes a neighbor-hood issue, and the neighbors band together to fight, through neighborhood walks and a vigil.

The Weirdo, by Theodore Taylor (Orlando, FL: Harcourt Brace Jovanovich, 1991; ad-vanced), is the story of Samantha Sanders and Chip Clewt, who work together to solve two murders and to extend a federal ban on hunting bears in the Powhatan, a National Wildlife Refuge. Their efforts include preparing posters, discussing their views at a public meeting, and providing testimony before government officials. Family conflicts (Samantha's father op-poses the hunting ban) and prejudice (Chip is disfigured as the result of a severe burn) are important elements of the story.

My Brother, My Sister, and I, by Yoko Kawashima Watkins (New York: Macmillan, 1994; advanced), is the incredible true story of three teenagers struggling to survive without their parents in post-World War II Japan. The obstacles that the three must overcome—poverty, homelessness, illness, prejudice, and false accusations of wrongdoing—will likely seem unbelievable to today's students, but the Kawashimas' resourcefulness and grit will help readers understand the capacity that people have to rise above the circumstances in which they find themselves.

Author Gloria Velasquez, in *Juanita Fights the School Board* (Houston, TX: Pinata Books, 1994), uses the alternating voices of 15-year-old Juanita and psychologist Sandra Martinez to explore issues of identity and acceptance. By helping Juanita when she is expelled for fighting, Dr. Martinez reaffirms her commitment to helping young people in the Chicano community. In the process, she comes to a new appreciation of her own family.

Gary Paulsen's *Nightjohn* (New York: Delacorte Press, 1993; advanced) tells a brutal story of how slaves were treated in the 1850s. Yet the determination of the title character to teach other slaves to read and write—and their determination to learn—is truly heroic. Even after Nightjohn escaped from the "master," he returned to run a secret night school. The idea that learning is worth risking one's life for should spark discussion among today's students, who often take school for granted.

While not all of these books are historical, they can provide a stimulant for discussing the qualities that everyday heroes and national heroes, such as those written about in biographies, have in common. A group of students, each of whom has read a different book about an everyday hero, might compare the characters in their books and create a special magazine to honor "everyday heroes" or "people who make a difference" (*Newsweek* recently carried such a feature). They could include characters in books, people from history, and people they know.

6. Events Have Multiple, Complex Causes; Some Causes May Be Nonrational and/or Accidental.

Much of historical research and writing has to do with the search for explanations, with explaining why something happened and what consequences resulted. Often, both the causes and consequences are multiple and complex. Students may have difficulty understanding that the causes of events were not readily apparent at the time the event occurred and that some causes are nonrational and accidental. Furthermore, they may confuse a correlation between two events with a cause-effect relationship.

To develop the ideas represented in this theme, students need opportunities to talk about the causes and consequences of events that they read about, in their textbooks and in literary works. A story does not have to be sophisticated in order for students to analyze causes. For example, the book *Aurora Means Dawn*, by Scott Russell Sanders, illustrated by Jill Kastner (New York: Bradbury Press, 1989; primary) tells about a family moving from Connecticut to Ohio in 1800. As they are approaching the area where they plan to settle, the family's wagon gets stuck in the mud. The causes of their problem include their decision to move west to find cheap land, a thunderstorm, stubborn oxen, and a narrow wagon trail cut through the forest. While the delay in the family's reaching their goal was only temporary, students can likely compare the situation to ones in which they have faced obstacles caused by the weather, physical surroundings, or actions of others.

The Story of Ruby Bridges, by Robert Coles, illustrated by George Ford (New York: Scholastic, 1995; primary) is the moving story of a first-grade child who is the first African-American student at a New Orleans elementary school. Many factors can be cited as causes of Ruby's experience. Her family's economic problems led to their move to New Orleans when Ruby was four. National law and a federal judge's decision led to the desegregation order. The prejudice of white parents, the religious beliefs of Ruby's family, and the concern of Ruby's teacher all shaped her actual school experience, which many of today's students will find incredible. How people's actions and responses are shaped by religious beliefs or other beliefs about right and wrong can be a topic for class discussion. What beliefs caused Ruby's family to decide she should be the first black student to attend the school? What beliefs caused white protesters to behave the way they did? What beliefs caused Miss Hurley to act as she did? How can beliefs cause people to act in both positive and negative ways?

Peppe the Lamplighter, by Elisa Bartone, illustrated by Ted Lewin (New York: Lothrop, Lee & Shepard, 1993; primary) is a story illustrating complex causes based on human emotions. Because their father is ill and their mother is dead, the children in Peppe's family, Italian immigrants in turn-of-the-century New York, must work. But Peppe's father says he is ashamed of Peppe's lamplighting job. The reasons for the father's feelings, as well as their effects on Peppe and the causes of the father's eventual change of heart, provide interesting material for student discussion.

The Sad Night: The Story of an Aztec Victory and a Spanish Loss, by Sally Schofer Mathews (New York: Clarion Books, 1994; primary, intermediate), is a nonfiction book that recounts the events leading to the last victory the Aztecs would enjoy over the Spaniards. Illustrated with ink and watercolors in the style of the Aztec codices, the book shows how wide-ranging factors contributed to the events of the "sad night." These factors included the Aztecs' belief system, political events in Spain, the greed of some Spaniards, the physical setting of Tenochtitlan, and the technologies used by both the Aztecs and Spaniards. Students may be interested to know that Mexican people today do not consider Moctezuma a hero; they believe he could have done more to keep Cortes from entering Mexico. On the other hand, they do see Cuauhtemoc, who succeeded Moctezuma, as a hero because he fought long and hard against Cortes and his forces. Do students think it is fair that Moctezuma is not respected by the modern-day people of his country? Are they judging him by today's standards, or by the knowledge that was available to him at the time?

The Clock, by James Lincoln Collier and Christopher Collier, illustrated by Kelly Maddox (New York: Delacorte Press, 1992; intermediate, advanced) deals with life in the textile mills of New England. While the financial irresponsibility of the heroine's father, greed, and regional economics are all factors in the story's events, the authors also look at the effect of a particular technology—the clock—in changing people's lives. Teachers could introduce the notion of the clock's impact on society by asking students to estimate how many times a day they check the time or are made aware of the time. Students could then use peel-off labels attached to their wrists to keep track of the actual number of times that they check or are made aware of the time in a 24-hour period. Discuss such questions as the following with students: How accurate were their guesses? Are they surprised at how often they check the time or are made aware of the time? What kinds of activities require them to know the time? How would life have been different before there were clocks? Do students think people were as aware of time before clocks were invented? After students have read the book, return to these questions and discuss the effect of the clock on how people's lives were structured and scheduled.

The title character in *Lyddie*, by Katherine Paterson (New York: Lodestar, 1991; advanced), is a 13-year-old girl who works in the mills of Lowell, Massachusetts, to pay her family's debts. The story's opening sentence—"The bear had been their undoing, though at the time they had all laughed"—is a clear indication that everything in Lyddie's life cannot be explained rationally. A bear's rampaging through their home was not the only reason the family left their farm, however; Lyddie's father decided to move west to seek his fortune, and her mother's mental instability caused her to seek refuge with relatives and to indenture Lyddie and her brother Charles to nearby merchants. The lives of the girls at Lowell, to which Lyddie eventually finds her way, are also influenced by numerous factors, including the textile companies' greed and society's morals and prejudices. Yet the girls, including Lyddie, maintain their ability to influence their own destiny by forming a union and taking action to help each other. The book provides rich material for discussion and student writing. For example, students might discuss factors that were most important in causing four of the main characters in the book to leave the mills—Amelia, Betsy, Prudence, and Lyddie herself. Why did Lyddie stay longer than the others? What motivated her actions? What external events finally caused her to leave the mill? Was her leaving inevitable when these events occurred, or could she have acted differently and thus stayed?

The Road to Memphis, by Mildred D. Taylor (New York: Dial Books, 1990; advanced) finds the author's fictional Logan family, featured in two earlier books, in 1941. The events that unfold in the tragic story have multiple causes, many of which are nonrational and some seemingly remote from the lives of the family members and their friends. Among the factors that influence events are racism, the onset of World War II, jealousy, passion, fear, and economic necessity. Pairs of students could pick individual characters from the book (the characters are numerous) and create posters showing changes in the character's life. The posters should show not only external events but also the individual's own decisions and actions that played a part in creating the changes. Different pairs of students may interpret the causes of events differently, which could lead to interesting discussions.

7. Geography and History Are Related.

Examining the five themes for teaching geography (*Guidelines for Geographic Education* 1984) can elucidate the links between geography and history. In particular, the geographic themes of relationships within places, movement, and region provide a framework for looking at the relationship of geography and history.

The theme of relationships within places looks at the interactions between humans and the environment. These relationships have three significant aspects (Hill and McCormick 1989):

- How people depend on the environment.
- How people adapt to the environment.
- How people change the environment.

All of these aspects are as relevant to historical study as they are to analysis of the present.

Movement refers to all kinds of human interactions between and among places. As described in the *Guidelines for Geographic Education,* "they [people in various places] travel from one place to another, they communicate with each other or they rely upon products, information, and ideas that come from beyond their immediate environment. Movement of people, products, information, and ideas has been important throughout history, as well as in the present."

The region is a concept developed by geographers to organize their data to make it manageable. A region is an "area that displays unity in terms of selected criteria." Regional differences have been important in both U.S. and world history.

While it can be useful to focus on one or two of the geographic themes in developing students' understanding of the relationship of geography and history, the relationship can also be examined more holistically. Both approaches are represented in our discussion of specific books below.

Because it involves a unique setting (the banks of the Hudson River) and use of the environment (cutting ice from the frozen river to sell in New York City), *The Ice Horse*, by Candace Christiansen, illustrated by Thomas Locker (New York: Dial Books, 1993; primary), provides a means of looking at the relationship between people and the environment. When students have read the book, ask them to look for evidence of how people depended on, adapted to, and changed the environment in this story.

The many books about settlement of the West by Anglo settlers provide opportunities to explore this idea as well. For example, *Going West*, by Jean Van Leeuwen, illustrated by Thomas B. Allen (New York: Dial Books, 1992; primary) tells the story of a family moving West in the 1800s. Because the book ends with the line "And our house felt like home," the story provides a good stimulant for discussing whether people need to make some adaptations in the environment in order to feel at home in a place. Is this true in all times and all places? Encourage students to explain their answers using examples from their own experience, as well as from a variety of books they have read.

Giants in the Land, by Diana Applebaum, illustrated by Michael McCurdy (Boston: Houghton Mifflin, 1993; primary, intermediate) tells of the cutting of the giant pines of New England for use as masts for the ships of the British Royal Navy. The trees were a product that was moved because people had traveled to New England and discovered this resource but also because people in Britain wanted the capability to move their forces faster than had been possible with other ships. In the process of cutting the trees, of course, people also changed the environment, making the book suitable for discussing the relationships theme as well as the movement theme.

Another book that develops understanding of multiple themes is *Skylark*, by Patricia MacLachlan (New York: HarperCollins, 1994; intermediate), the sequel to the popular *Sarah, Plain and Tall*. In this book, Sarah and the children Anna and Caleb are forced to leave their prairie home because of severe drought. The story makes clear the adaptations people make in new environments, as well as the differences between regions. A different response to another geographically related problem faced by settlers in the West can be found in *Clouds of Terror*, by Catherine Welch, illustrated by Laurie K. Johnson (Minneapolis: Carolrhoda Books, 1994; intermediate). The father's decision to leave the homestead to find work can be compared to Sarah's decision to take the children from the farm in *Skylark*.

Because the United States is both a nation of immigrants and a highly mobile society, life stories can be a useful vehicle for studying movement. Students can be exposed to the idea of pushes and pulls; that is, people sometimes move because something in their current environment pushes them out while other times they are drawn or pulled to a new place by potential benefits. Students might map moves of the subject of a biography, using different colors or symbols to indicate whether each move was caused by a push or pull. Such a technique can be used even with easy biographies, such as *Alvin Ailey*, by Andrea Davis Pinkney, illustrated by Brian Pinkney (New York: Hyperion, 1993; primary, intermediate). It can also be applied to a more difficult biography, such as *Ruth Bader Ginsburg: Fire and Steel on the Supreme Court*, by Eleanor H. Ayer (New York: Dillon Press, 1994; intermediate, advanced). In creating their maps, older students might also show the movement of the subject's ideas. In Ginsburg's case, students could create symbols showing dissemination of ideas through publishing, teaching, and court decisions.

Fictional works for all levels of students also deal with migration and can be analyzed in a similar fashion. For example, students could read *When Jo Louis Won the Title*, by Belinda Rochelle, illustrated by Larry Johnson (Boston: Houghton Mifflin, 1994; primary, intermediate) and discuss why Jo's grandfather moved to New York and why that move was important to the family for several generations.

African-American migration from the South to the North in the early years of the 20th-century is also the topic of the marvelous book *The Great Migration: An American Story*, paintings and text by Jacob Lawrence, with a poem in appreciation by Walter Dean Myers (New York: HarperCollins, 1993; all ages). This book presents Lawrence's series of paintings on the migration of black Americans, accompanied by an introduction that describes his own family's migration and how he came to understand his own experiences in the larger historical context. Simple explanations accompany the paintings, which are followed by Myers's poem. As Lawrence says, "migration means movement," and his brilliant paintings can help students better understand not only why people move, but the consequences of that movement.

Students can discover how people in different regions experienced historical events differently by comparing books set in the same time period but different regions. For example, Mildred D. Taylor's *Mississippi Bridge* (New York: Dial Books, 1990; intermediate, advanced) and Phyllis Rossiter's *Moxie* (New York: Four Winds, 1990; intermediate, advanced) both deal with young people's experiences in the Depression, with poverty and the effects of weather being common themes; the specifics of the characters' experiences, however, are influenced by the region in which they live (as well as by their race). Ann Turnbull's *Speedwell* (Cambridge, MA: Candlewick Press, 1992; intermediate, advanced), which is set in England during the Depression, and Jackie French Koller's *Nothing to Fear* (San Diego: Gulliver Books, 1991; advanced) set in New York City, would provide an even broader comparison across regions.

Patricia Beatty has written a number of books about the Civil War, set in various parts of the United States. Three of her books are *Who Comes with Cannons?* (New York: Morrow, 1992; advanced), *Jayhawker* (New York: Morrow, 1991; advanced), and *Turn Homeward, Hannalee* (New York: Morrow, 1984; advanced). Since each book is set in a different state, reading all three would provide a perspective on the link between geography and history.

Toning the Sweep, by Angela Johnson (New York: Orchard Books, 1993; intermediate, advanced) weaves a complex story of three generations of women in an African-American family and their relationship to the environments in which they live. As the three women prepare to move the grandmother from her home in the California desert to her daughter's Midwestern apartment, the granddaughter Emily videotapes the experience and reflects on her family's history and geography—why her mother and grandmother abruptly left the South when her grandfather was killed in a racially motivated murder, why she and her grandmother love the desert and her mother hates it (a difference that is representative of a deeper friction between her mother and grandmother), why her grandmother has brought kudzu from her native South to the desert, and why her mother has moved so often and sometimes seems so sad and angry. The family and geographic relationships are complex and well worth student discussion. Could something cause students to want to leave their home immediately? How would they feel if one of their parents wanted to move abruptly? What might they take with them to grow in the new environment? What plants in their community were, in fact, brought by settlers from other places? Can feelings about a place be tied up with feelings about events in our lives?

8. We Construct Our Knowledge of the Past by Asking Questions, Seeking Information from Many Sources, and Sorting, Evaluating, and Analyzing the Information.

This theme, which involves understanding the work of the historian, includes many aspects: the recognition and use of historical questions, the use of a wide variety of sources, and the analysis of information.

Most students would probably say that "What happened when?" is the question historians ask, not recognizing that historians also seek to explain why things happened and the consequences they had. Thus, being able to create more complex historical questions and to recognize the questions behind the works they read are important skills.

The use and exploration of historical questions is not evident in a great number of children's books, but there are a few exceptions. One such exception is *Home Place*, by Crescent Dragonwagon, illustrated by Jerry Pinkney (New York: Macmillan, 1990; primary). In this story, which is illustrated with lovely pencil and watercolor drawings, a family out hiking sees daffodils growing in a secluded spot in the woods. They begin wondering why the daffodils grow there. As they explore, they find clues to the family that once lived in this spot and they begin to imagine the lives that unfolded there. Not only does the book suggest how an interesting anomaly can prompt historical questions, it also shows how much fun discovering the past can be.

Another book that explores historical questions and the fun of answering them is *The Keepsake Chest*, by Katharine Wilson Precek (New York: Macmillan, 1992; intermediate, advanced). The main character, Meg Hamilton, finds an old trunk in the attic of the family's new home in Ohio. Intrigued by the contents of the attic, she begins asking questions and seeking information about the previous residents of the house. She talks with an older neighbor who knew the previous residents, visits the historical society and talks to a historian, and searches through census and other public records. The book not only illustrates the process of "doing history," but the excitement of finding the answers to historical questions. When students have read and discussed this book, you might present them with a historical artifact from your community, asking them to formulate questions about the artifact. When they have listed several questions, divide the class into groups, assigning each group one of the questions, for which the group is to develop a strategy they might use to find an answer. Encourage them to consider a variety of sources from which they might seek information.

With respect to the wide variety of sources available for studying history, this book focuses primarily on literature as a source. Use of literature certainly moves students away from their reliance on the traditional textbook and encyclopedia. Yet students must learn how to evaluate historical information in a work of literature by comparing it with other sources. Thus, having artifacts, diaries, letters, photographs, and other primary source materials available for student use in conjunction with works of literature is highly recommended.

Through the use of literature, students can also learn how other sources are used by writers to create historical fiction, biographies, or other literary works. Thus, we recommend exposing students to literature based on or incorporating a variety of primary sources. For example, Ann Turner's *Nettie's Trip South*, illustrated by Ronald Himler (New York: Macmillan, 1987; intermediate), is based on a young girl's diary. In the diary, Nettie (who was Turner's great-grandmother) described a train trip from Albany, New York, to Richmond, Virginia. On the trip, Nettie witnessed a slave auction, an experience that profoundly affected her. Through discussion of this moving book, students can be helped to see how such personal accounts as diaries provide historians with insights not only into what happened in the past but how events affected people on various levels, including the emotional level.

A different kind of journal, one meant to provide information, is the basis for *Off the Map: The Journals of Lewis and Clark*, edited by Peter and Connie Roop, illustrated by Tim Tanner (New York: Walker, 1993; intermediate). Students could compare this book with *Nettie's Trip South* to get a sense of the different reasons that particular kinds of historical material are created and how that affects the way the material is used. For example, which type of journal gives more information about specific dates and peoples? Which helps you better understand how people felt about events?

Older students might analyze books that are based on writings by the subject but are presented in another form. For example, *Across America on an Emigrant Train*, by Jim Murphy (New York: Clarion Books, 1993; advanced) recounts Robert Louis Stevenson's trip from Scotland to California to join the woman he loved. While the book is based primarily on Stevenson's own journal, the author has not simply reprinted the journal but has written a historical narrative to place the journal in context. What historical questions do students think the author was trying to answer? Why did he choose to write the book as he did? Does the author's choice make the book more interesting or less interesting than a simple reprint of the journal? More informative or less informative? More accurate or less accurate? Encourage students to justify their answers to these questions, to which there are certainly no "correct" answers.

Another book to which upper elementary students could apply this kind of analysis is *Letters from a Slave Girl: The Story of Harriet Jacobs*, by Mary E. Lyons (New York: Scribners, 1992; advanced). Lyons has used Jacobs's own account of her life, plus other sources, to create fictional letters that Jacobs might have written as she tried to escape from slavery. The author's note at the end of the book provides interesting insights into the author's work in, in her words, "reimagining Harriet's life." Why the author would describe her work as reimagining could provoke an interesting discussion of the process of writing about a person who lived many years ago.

Other books could be used to help students explore art as a historical source. For example, *Stitching Stars: The Story Quilts of Harriet Powers*, by Mary E. Lyons (New York: Scribner's, 1993; intermediate, advanced), introduces young people to the idea that folk arts, such as quilts, are a source of information about the past. The author's analysis of the quilts themselves and other information about their creator can serve as a model for students of how to ask questions and draw conclusions about historical artifacts.

Memoirs and oral histories appropriate for students' use are also available. Students can compare information from such sources with other sources on the same topics, such as textbooks, evaluating when they think the firsthand accounts are more and less reliable than writings by historians or textbook authors. This kind of comparison/evaluation of sources can help students see that all sources, including textbooks, have a point of view. Wrestling with conflicting accounts of an event can also help students understand point of view and multiple perspectives.

On some topics, several memoirs or collections of oral histories are available, allowing students to compare and contrast the recollections of several people who lived through the same events and to grapple with how to evaluate the accuracy of such accounts. One example of such a topic is the Holocaust and the Jewish children who were hidden and thus survived to tell of their experiences. For example, Nelly S. Toll has written *Behind the Secret Window: A Memoir of a Hidden Childhood During World War Two* (New York: Dial Books, 1993; advanced), which is illustrated with her own paintings created while in hiding in Lwow, Poland. This fascinating book-length account could be compared with shorter oral histories or fictionalized accounts based on true stories. Such sources include *The Hidden Children*, by Howard Greenfeld (New York: Ticknor and Fields, 1993; advanced); *Young People Speak: Surviving the Holocaust in Hungary*, compiled and edited by Andrew Handler and Susan V. Meschel (New York: Watts, 1993; advanced); *Echoes of World War II*, by Trish Marx (New York: Lerner, 1994; advanced); *Jacob's Rescue: A Holocaust Story*, by Malka Drucker and Michael Halperin (New York: Bantam Doubleday Dell, 1993; advanced); and *Daniel's Story*, by Carol Matas (New York: Scholastic, 1993; advanced).

As students learn about the variety of sources used by historians, they will begin to see that sources conflict and that writing historical narrative requires comparing and sorting data, drawing conclusions about what data is most reliable, and constructing explanations based upon their conclusions. Asking students to consider why things happened and to explain their answers will help them begin constructing historical explanations. Opportunities to write historical narratives will develop these skills even further.

Writing historical narrative is an example of activities that involve students in "doing history" related to events or people they have read about. Such activities are particularly helpful with respect to understanding this theme. An excellent book for students that encourages them to become involved in doing history (in a fun way) is *My Backyard History Book*, by David Weitzman, illustrated by James Robertson (Boston: Little, Brown, 1975; intermediate, advanced). Despite the copyright date, this book is still in print at the time of this writing.

A number of resources especially useful in developing students' understanding of this theme are reviewed in Porter (1994).

References

Bradley Commission on History in the Schools, *Building a History Curriculum: Guidelines for Teaching History in Schools* (Washington, DC: Educational Excellence Network, 1988).

Cheney, Lynn, *American Memory: A Report on the Humanities in the Nation's Public Schools* (Washington, DC: National Endowment for the Humanities, 1987).

Guidelines for Geographic Education: Elementary and Secondary School (Washington, DC: American Association of Geographers, and Macomb, IL: National Council for Geographic Education, 1984).

Hill, A. David, and Regina McCormick, *Geography: A Resource Book for Secondary Schools* (Santa Barbara, CA: ABC-CLIO, 1989).

History-Social Science Framework for California Public Schools (Sacramento, CA: California State Department of Education, 1988).

Lessons from History: Essential Understandings and Historical Perspectives Students Should Acquire (Los Angeles: National Center for History in the Schools, 1992).

Porter, Priscilla H., "The Student as Historian," *Social Studies and the Young Learner* (November/December 1994), pp. 23-26.

MODEL GUIDES FOR USING CHILDREN'S LITERATURE IN HISTORY

Characteristics of a Good Guide

Susan Hepler has identified several characteristics for quality guides for literature-based programs. First, she says that "A good guide should improve the quality of the reader's experience with the book....Through talk, readers should be able to say, 'I hadn't thought about that before,' or 'I had, but I couldn't put it into words.'" A good guide should also include questions that cause students to "examine why people act as they do" and, in moderation, "encourage readers to identify with whatever aspects of the text match their perceptions." Finally, a good guide should include activities that "serve the reader and the book first, not some particular curriculum area."

In developing the guides included here, we have attempted to apply these criteria. Thus, although we emphasize historic understanding, we do not focus exclusively on history. For each book, we include at least some questions that, like those used in the Great Books program, have "no single right answers, requiring both the student and teacher to examine factual information, assess motivation, and make inferences" (Gallagher 1991).

Many of the books will be most effective if read aloud, especially with younger students. Having several copies of the book may still be a good idea, however, to allow close examination of the illustrations. For primary grade students, we include a relatively small number of questions in each guide. For older students, the number of questions increases, and we divide the list of questions by chapter or section of the book.

The chart on the next page lists the books for which guides are provided, appropriate grade levels, and historic understandings addressed. The understandings (abbreviated) are:

1. Real people experienced past events and issues.

2. The past is important in our lives and to our culture.

3. Change and continuity are both natural parts of the human story.

4. People throughout history were different but also had many things in common.

5. Individuals have made a difference in history, for both good and ill.

6. Events have multiple, complex causes.

7. Geography and history are related.

8. We construct our knowledge of the past.

References

Gallagher, Arlene F., ed., *Acting Together: Excerpts from Children's Literature on Themes from the Constitution* (Boulder, CO: Social Science Education Consortium, 1991).

Hepler, Susan, "A Guide for the Teacher Guides: Doing It Yourself," *The New Advocate* (Summer 1988).

Title	Grade Level	Historical Understandings*							
		1	2	3	4	5	6	7	8
Grandfather's Journey	K-2	X	X					X	
In America	K-3	X	X	X					
The Bracelet	K-3	X		X				X	
The Lily Cupboard	1-3	X				X	X		
Katie's Trunk	1-3	X			X		X		
An Ellis Island Christmas	1-3	X			X		X		
Li'l Sis and Uncle Willie	2-4	X	X		X			X	X
Teammates	2-4			X	X	X			
Doesn't Fall Off His Horse	2-4		X	X	X			X	
Family Pictures	2-4		X	X	X			X	
Dinner at Aunt Connie's House	3-5		X			X			X
From Miss Ida's Porch	3-5		X	X		X			
Christmas in the Big House, Christmas in the Quarters	3-5	X		X	X				X
Guests	3-5	X	X	X	X				X
My Daniel	4-6	X		X			X	X	X
Dear Levi	4-6	X				X	X	X	
Steal Away Home	4-6	X					X	X	X
White Lilacs	5-6	X	X		X		X	X	
Dragon's Gate	5-6	X				X	X	X	
A Break with Charity	5-6	X		X	X	X	X		X

*See page 31 for listing of historical understandings.

Grandfather's Journey,
written and illustrated by Allen Say
(Boston: Houghton Mifflin, 1993).

Summary

In this Caldecott Medal winner, Allen Say tells of his grandfather's travels around the United States as a young immigrant. After returning to Japan to raise his family, the grandfather regales young Allen with stories of California, where Allen later settles. Like his grandfather, Allen finds that whenever he is in either California or Japan, he is homesick for the other.

Initiating Activities

1. Tell students that family stories are one important way that we learn about the past. Have students share family stories they have heard from older family members, either in pairs or as a large group (taking two or three volunteers). Discuss with students why they like to hear these stories. Possible answers include because they are funny, they help students understand what older family members were like as young people, sharing the stories makes the family feel closer, the stories help students understand why their family lives where and how it does.

2. Next, ask students whether family stories can help them understand historical events that affected many people. Help them identify examples of stories that are linked to larger events, such as a relative's involvement in the Vietnam War or Civil Rights movement. Tell students that Allen Say has written a book entitled *Grandfather's Journey*. It recounts stories told to Allen by his grandfather about an experience many Americans have had—coming to the United States from another country. Show the cover illustration and allow students to speculate on where Allen's grandfather came from, how old he was when he made the journey, and so on.

Discussion Questions

1. What words does Allen Say use to describe his grandfather's reactions to the United States? Do these words help you understand how the grandfather felt? Have you ever felt that way when you experienced a new place?

2. Were you surprised that Allen's grandfather decided to return to Japan? Why or why not? How do you think his daughter felt about the move? Does the story give you any clues about how the daughter felt? Explain your answer.

3. What happened to keep Allen's grandfather from making a visit to California? In what other ways did the war affect Allen's grandfather?

4. Do you think the grandfather's stories had an effect on Allen? If so, how do you think they affected him? What do you think Allen means when he says "I think I know my grandfather now."

Follow-up Activities

1. Have students make a book retelling and illustrating one of their family stories. Encourage them to include a reference to a major historical event that influenced the people in the story; to do so, they will probably need to ask family members questions to get more details about their story. If students cannot think of a family story to illustrate, suggest some questions that they can ask their parents or grandparents to gather a story:

- How did you and (mom, dad, grandma, grandpa) meet?

- What happened on the day I was born?

- What was the most embarrassing (funniest, scariest, most interesting) thing that ever happened to you as a child?

- Do you remember what you were doing when President Kennedy was shot (or when another memorable event occurred)?

- Have you seen the Vietnam Veterans Memorial? What does it remind you of?

2. Encourage students to read other stories about immigrants and their journeys. *My Grandmother's Journey*, by John Cech, illustrated by Sharon McGinley-Nally (New York: Gulliver Books, 1991), tells the story of a woman who flees Russia, only to be forced to work in a German factory during World War II. After the war, the family finally arrived in the United States. *How Many Days to America?*, by Eve Bunting, illustrated by Beth Peck (New York: Clarion, 1988), tells the story of modern refugees, fleeing their Caribbean home by boat. The hardships faced by the people in these two stories should prompt students to consider what motivates people to leave their homelands.

3. Organize the students into small groups and provide each group with travel or news magazines to search through for pairs of pictures of Allen and grandfather's two homes—Japan and California. The pictures should show differences between the two places or aspects of the two places that would appeal to students.

In America,
written and illustrated by Marissa Moss
(New York: Dutton, 1994).

Summary

As Walter and his Grandpa walk to the post office to mail a birthday present to his brother in Lithuania, Grandpa tells Walter why he decided to come to America while his brother chose not to move. As Walter listens to the story, he wonders if he could ever be as brave as his grandfather was as a small boy. The author has illustrated the book so that the drawings of Grandpa's stories suggest pictures in a photo album.

Initiating Activities

1. Ask students to imagine all the things that would be different if they moved to another country. List their responses on the chalkboard. Ask: Would it be difficult to cope with so many changes? Would they be scared if they faced so many changes? Allow time for student discussion. Next, ask students to consider what reason might be powerful enough to cause them to face the changes and uncertainties involved in moving to another country.

2. Read the title and dedication of the book aloud to students. What do they think this book is about? What reason does the author suggest for why people are willing to face problems to move to America?

Discussion Questions

1. Where did Grandpa live before he came to America? Find Lithuania on a map. Trace the route from Lithuania, across Europe, across the Atlantic Ocean, and across the United States, as Grandpa described. Where do you think Walter and his Grandpa lived?

2. Why did Grandpa decide to come to America? Why didn't he have freedom in Lithuania? What do you think Grandpa meant when he said "Sometimes they (people) are scared of what they don't understand. And when they're scared, they can be mean." Can you think of times people have been mean because they were scared of what they didn't understand?

3. Why didn't Herschel want to move to America? Do you think he was really afraid there wouldn't be prunes in America? What does Grandpa think Herschel was afraid of? Do you agree? Why or why not?

4. Why did Walter decide to cross the street by himself? Do you think crossing the street by himself helped Walter answer the question of whether he would stay home like Herschel or travel to America like Grandpa? Which would you do?

5. Were you surprised when you learned what Grandpa was sending Herschel as a birthday present? Why or why not? Do you think prunes were a good choice? Explain your answer.

Follow-up Activities

1. Assign students to make a detailed comparison of the illustrations that show Grandpa's life in America with those that show his earlier days in Lithuania. Have them create lists of similarities and differences between the two places. What do they think the most important similarity is? What is the most important difference?

2. Suggest that students ask their parents to see pictures of their mother and father when they were young. What stories accompany the pictures?

3. Have students find out where their families came from originally. Display this information on a world map.

The Bracelet,

by Yoshiko Uchida, illustrated by Joanna Yardley (New York: Philomel Books, 1993).

Summary

The day she leaves for an internment camp, Emi receives a bracelet from her best friend. Although she vows never to take it off, in the first frightening day at a racetrack turned into a camp, Emi somehow loses the bracelet. Emi's mother helps her realize that she can remember her friend without the bracelet, just as they can remember their father, who has been sent to a prisoner of war camp in Montana, without their picture of him.

Initiating Activities

1. Ask students to think about a gift they have received that has been especially meaningful to them. What made the gift special? Do they still have the gift? Does it remind them of a special person, place, or event? Do they need the actual gift to remember that person, place, or event?

2. Show students the cover illustration. Why might the girl in the picture have a numbered tag on her coat? What is she sitting on? What is the person standing behind her holding? What do students think is happening in this picture?

Discussion Questions

1. What was happening to Emi's family? Why do you think the government was forcing them to move? How was where they lived related to being forced to move? Do you think the government's actions were fair? Why or why not? How would you feel if your country did not trust you?

2. Why do you think the author said the house was "like a gift box with no gift inside"? Does this phrase help you understand how Emi felt about seeing her house empty? Why do you think Emi kept trying to remember how the house looked when it was full of the family's things?

3. What did Emi's friend Laurie do to show that she would miss Emi? Do you think these were good ways to express her feelings? Have you ever had a friend move away? What did you do to show how you felt?

4. Why do you think each person could only take two suitcases? What do you think happened to all the family's other belongings? Remember that families did not have much time between the announcement that they would be forced to go to camps and actually leaving for the camps. If you could only take two suitcases to a camp where you might have to live for several years, what would you take?

5. Describe what happened once the family got to the center. How did Emi feel? Do you think you would have been scared if you had been there?

6. Describe the racetrack where the family had to stay. Why do you think the government chose a racetrack as a place for people to stay? How do you think staying in a place built for animals would make people feel?

7. How did Emi feel when she lost her bracelet? Do you think Emi felt worse because she was losing so many things at the same time? How did her mother help her feel better about losing the bracelet?

Follow-up Activities

1. Read the "Afterword" and discuss the internment of Japanese-Americans with students. Does Emi's story help them understand what being interned was like for Japanese-Americans? Why or why not?

2. In 1992, President Bush signed a bill creating a national monument at Manzanar. Ask students to design a monument that would pay tribute to the experiences of Japanese-American children like Emi and her sister.

3. You might want to read sections of *Farewell to Manzanar*, by Jeanne Wakatsuki Houston and James D. Houston (Boston: Houghton Mifflin, 1973), to students. This book is a first-person account by a woman who lived in the camps as a child. It also describes the prejudice that Japanese-Americans faced when they returned to schools attended by Anglo students after the war. Students could also examine Ansel Adam's photographs of the camp, which are included in *Manzanar*, by John Armor and Peter Wright (New York: Times Books, 1988). The photos reveal the stark landscape, emptiness, and loneliness of the camp but also the determination of the Japanese-Americans to survive and thrive. You could also share the poem "In Response to Executive Order 9066," by Dwight Okita, reprinted in *Celebrate America in Poetry and Art*, edited by Nora Panzer (New York: Hyperion Books, 1994), which tells the story of a less open-minded best friend.

4. Students could compare Emi's experience with that of the narrator in the book *Time to Go*, by Beverly and David Fiday, illustrated by Thomas B. Allen (Orlando, FL: Harcourt Brace Jovanovich, 1990). This boy's family is being forced to leave its farm because of economic reasons. Although the reasons for leaving are different, many of the feelings experienced by the two children are the same. Both try to hang on to their homes by remembering them in better times. Ask if any students in the class have moved and encourage them to share the reasons for the move and the feelings associated with moving.

© 1995 Social Science Education Consortium

Summary

Set in Holland during World War II, this book tells the story of a young Jewish girl named Miriam, whose parents send her to stay with a farm family. When soldiers come to the farm, Miriam must hide in a cupboard whose latch is hidden by a lily painted on the wall.

Initiating Activities

1. Read the first page of the book to students. On a world map, locate Holland and Germany and discuss what it means to invade another country. Let students speculate on what it would be like to live in a country that had been invaded by an enemy nation.

2. Show students the illustrations on the cover and first page of the book. Do the pictures look like they are of a country that has been invaded? Why or why not? Given the introduction and these pictures, can students make any guesses about what the story is going to be about?

Discussion Questions

1. Why did Miriam's parents send her to the country? Give as many reasons as you can.

2. How did Miriam feel about being sent to the country? How do you think you would have felt in her place?

3. Describe the lily cupboard. Why was it important? How would Miriam know when it was time to go to the lily cupboard?

4. How did Nello's family try to make Miriam feel at home on their farm? Were these good ideas? Do you have any other ideas for helping her feel at home?

5. Why didn't Miriam run to the lily cupboard when she heard someone whistling "Frere Jacques"? Why was taking the bunny with her so important to Miriam?

6. Do you think Nello's father and mother were heroes? Explain your answer.

Follow-up Activities

1. Encourage students to write letters from Miriam to her parents, describing her experiences on Nello's family farm. In their letters, students should give their opinions about Nello's family.

2. If students have read Yoshiko Uchida's book, *The Bracelet*, students could compare and contrast the two relocation experiences. What feelings and experiences did Emi and Miriam share? What feelings and experiences were different? Encourage students to decide on a pet that might have given Emi the comfort Miriam found in the rabbit. Students could draw the pet and pick an appropriate name for it.

Katie's Trunk,
by Ann Turner, illustrated by Ron Himler
(New York: Macmillan, 1992).

Summary

The title character's parents are Tories in the days before the American Revolution. Because they do not agree with their neighbors, they have lost many friends. When rebels come to their house looking for money and supplies, Katie hides in a trunk. One of the men finds her, but distracts the others and leaves the lid of the trunk up, allowing her to breathe. His actions help her realize that there is good even in those who have opposing views.

Initiating Activities

1. Remind students that the United States was once part of Great Britain. The nation earned its freedom in the American Revolution, in which Americans fought the British. Who were the heroes of the Revolution? Who was the enemy?

2. Tell students that not everyone who lived in the American colonies wanted to be free of British rule. These people were called Tories. Ask students to imagine that their family is a Tory family; almost everyone else in the town they live in is a "rebel." What might life be like for the Tories? Who, from their point of view, is the enemy? Explain that the family in the book students are about to read is in this situation.

Discussion Questions

1. What was making Katie's family skittish or itchy? Do the first few pictures in the book help you understand the family's feelings? Why or why not? Have you ever had the feeling that a "sour rain" was about to fall? What caused the feeling? Did the feeling affect the way you behaved?

2. Why had the family lost their friends? Do you think it is fair for children to lose their friends because of what their parents believe? Explain your answer. When people hissed "Tory" at Katie and her sister and brother and they saw people marching about with weapons, how do you think they felt? Why do you think they remained Tories even though they lost their friends?

3. Why did the family hide in the woods? Why did Katie run back to the house? If you had a chance to tell Katie what you thought of her actions, what would you say?

4. Describe what happened while Katie was in the trunk. Why do you think John Warren protected Katie? Do you think he would have done the same thing if he had found Katie's father hiding in the trunk? Why or why not?

5. What do you think Katie meant when she said "He'd left one seam of goodness there, and we were all tied to it: Papa, Mama, Walter, Hattie and me"?

6. Do you think Katie ever played with her friend Celia again? Why or why not?

Follow-up Activities

1. Ask students to draw pictures or write letters that Katie might give to her friend Celia. What would she want to say to or show Celia? How might Celia respond?

2. Ask students to think about the events in the story from the perspective of Katie's friend Celia. What would Celia say about losing Katie as a friend? If Celia shared her father's desire for independence from Great Britain, how would she feel about the events taking place—would she be scared, excited, mad? Encourage students to write a brief story from Celia's point of view.

An Ellis Island Christmas,
by Maxinne Rhea Leighton,
illustrated by Dennis Nolan
(New York: Penguin Group, 1992).

Summary

The immigrant experience is the focus of this book, which tells of a Polish family's journey to America. Krysia feels excitement, fear, sadness, seasickness, and affection for shipboard friends as she and her mother and two brothers journey to meet her father, who traveled ahead of them to find work and a home.

Initiating Activities

1. Ask students where their families originally came from. Do they know how their family members traveled to the United States? Make a list of all of the forms of transportation that family members may have used to come to the United States.

2. Tell students that they are going to be reading a story about a family that traveled to the United States. One way that they traveled was by foot. Show the cover illustration and ask students to speculate on what other method of transportation they used? Point out the title of the book and ask students if they know where Ellis Island is. If no one knows, again ask them to speculate on its location based on the cover illustration.

Discussion Questions

1. Why was Krysia's family moving? Why did the father go ahead of the rest of the family? How did Krysia feel about the move? Do you think you would have felt the same way?

2. Describe conditions on the ship. What would have been hardest for you to get used to? What helped Krysia get used to life on the ship? Do you think conditions on a ship would be different for immigrants today? Why or why not?

3. How does Krysia feel when she sees the Statue of Liberty? Explain what she means when she says "I could see America better now. Many people. Many faces. Many songs."

4. Describe Ellis Island and what happened to the woman with the "E". Do you think it was fair to turn people away because they were sick? Why or why not?

5. What happened with the banana? Have you ever had a new food that you did not know how to eat? Describe what happened.

6. What tradition did Krysia learn was shared by children in Poland and the United States? How was the tradition practiced differently in the two countries? How do you think

it made Krysia feel to learn that some traditions from her home country were practiced in her new country, too?

Follow-up Activities

1. Read "About This Book" with the students. Challenge students to use evidence from this section and elsewhere in the book (the 48 stars on the flag indicates that the events occurred after 1912, when Arizona became the 48th state) to determine about when the events in the book occurred.

2. Invite a recent immigrant to the United States to talk about how immigrating today is similar to and different from immigrating in the early years of the century. How did this immigrant travel? What kinds of processing occurred when he/she arrived in the United States? Did he/she know before coming that he/she would be allowed to stay, or was there concern that he/she might be turned away? Did he/she find that some traditions from their home country were also practiced in the United States? Was this surprising? Why or why not? Did he/she encounter any new foods? How many belongings was he/she able to bring? After the visit, students could write and illustrate a book about the visitor's experiences.

3. For younger students, mount a large picture of the Statue of Liberty on posterboard and encourage students to write "describing" words around the picture to tell what the statue means to them and to other Americans.

Li'l Sis and Uncle Willie,
by Gwen Everett, illustrated with the paintings
of William H. Johnson
(New York: Rizzoli, 1991).

Summary

This book is based on events in the life of artist William Johnson, whose vibrant paintings illustrate the story. Johnson, the Uncle Willie of the title, has lived in New York and Europe. His visit to the family home in South Carolina delights his relatives, especially Li'l Sis, who loves Uncle Willie's stories of the people and places depicted in his paintings. Although World War II and other events prevent Li'l Sis from visiting Uncle Willie in Europe and New York, his letters and snapshots of his work help Li'l Sis develop pride in being African American.

Initiating Activities

1. Ask students if they can remember a visit from a family member who lives somewhere far away. Was the visit exciting? Did the family member have stories to share about the places he or she had visited or lived?

2. Show students the title page and read the subtitle of the book ("A Story Based on the Life and Paintings of William H. Johnson") to students. Based on the subtitle, who do they think Uncle Willie might be? What kind of work do they think he did? Is there any evidence besides the subtitle? (The picture shows him holding a paintbrush.)

Discussion Questions

1. Where does the story take place? Where were some of the places Uncle Willie had lived? Show these places on a map.

2. When do you think the story took place? Look for clues as we read the book to determine whether you are right.

3. Why did Uncle Willie like the city better than the small Southern town in which he grew up? What do the paintings tell you about his views of city and country life?

4. What did Aunt Della tell Li'l Sis about New York? Do you think Aunt Della had the same opinions about country and city life as Uncle Willie? Why or why not? If Uncle Willie and Aunt Della lived today, do you think they would feel the same way about country and city life? Why or why not?

5. What happened to make Europe unsafe for Uncle Willie and his wife Holcha? When did this happen?

6. What did the paintings that Uncle Willie sent Li'l Sis snapshots of show? Why do you think Uncle Willie sent Li'l Sis pictures of these paintings? How did the pictures and Uncle Willie's letters make Li'l Sis feel? Do you think paintings are a good way to learn about our history? Why or why not?

Follow-up Activities

1. Assign students to write a letter to Uncle Willie about his art. In their letters, students should explain what they did and didn't like about his paintings. They should also reflect on how his paintings help them understand the past.

2. Encourage students to begin a scrapbook like the one Li'l Sis kept. The scrapbook could contain their own illustrations showing how various historical events affected their own family or community (whether ethnic or geographic), as well as places they have visited and people important to them.

Teammates,
by Peter Golenbock, illustrated by Paul Bacon
(Orlando, FL: Gulliver Books, 1990).

Summary

This book opens with a comparison of life in the Negro Leagues and the Major Leagues during the 1940s. It then focuses on Jackie Robinson's role as the first African American in Major League baseball. The humiliations heaped on Jackie by fans, other ballplayers, and segregated facilities are contrasted with Jackie's courage and that of teammate Pee Wee Reese, who showed public support for Robinson. Watercolors and historic photos illustrate the text.

Initiating Activities

1. Ask students if they have teammates. Broaden their thinking beyond sports to other situations in which they work in a team. With students, brainstorm what makes a person a good teammate.

2. Show students the cover of the book. What kind of team do they think this story is about?

Discussion Questions

1. How was life in the Negro Leagues the same and different from life in the Major Leagues? What accounted for the differences? In what ways was playing in either the Negro Leagues or Major Leagues like playing professional baseball today?

2. Why did the first black player in the Major Leagues have to be "one special man"? What characteristics did the man need? Do you know anyone who has those characteristics?

3. What were some of the problems Jackie faced? Do you think the hopes of African-American people could have created a problem for Jackie? If so, how?

4. What actions by Pee Wee Reese showed his courage and sense of fair play? How did he express his feelings about the way people treated Jackie? Have you ever seen someone express their views in this way? Did Pee Wee have the characteristics we listed for a good teammate?

5. Explain why you think each of the following people was or was not a hero:

   • Branch Rickey

   • Jackie Robinson

   • Pee Wee Reese

Follow-up Activities

1. Encourage students to analyze the illustrations in the book. What can they learn from the photos? the drawings? Which provides more information? Which makes them understand how Jackie and Pee Wee felt? Have students make baseball cards for Jackie and Pee Wee and display them around the room.

2. If possible, make a variety of baseball cards from 1945-1960 available for students to analyze. What changes in the game can be seen on the cards? What stayed the same? Students may be surprised to learn that the last team (the Boston Red Sox) was not integrated until 1959, 12 years after Jackie Robinson's debut. Students could construct a chronology of baseball's integration using baseball cards or facsimiles of trading cards. If you want to launch a more in-depth investigation of social issues related to baseball, students could consider the birthplaces of black and white players. If they have changed, why might that be true? The history of Latino players in the Major Leagues could also be traced using baseball cards.

3. You may want to share the following book, especially with more able learners—*American Events: The Negro Baseball Leagues*, by David K. Fremon (New York: Macmillan, 1994). The book provides additional historical photographs, as well as a great deal of information, including a look at the down side of baseball's integration—the demise of the black-owned franchises in the Negro Leagues. Another resource on this topic is *Black Diamond: The Story of the Negro Baseball Leagues*, by Patricia C. McKissack and Frederick McKissack, Jr. (New York: Scholastic, 1994). The PBS series on baseball, produced by Ken Burns, includes segments on the Negro Leagues, as well as a moving session on Jackie Robinson. Portions could be shown to the class in conjunction with their reading on this topic.

Doesn't Fall Off His Horse,
written and illustrated by Virginia A. Stroud
(New York: Dial Books, 1994).

Summary

In this retelling of a story from her Kiowa youth, the author introduces young readers to the concept of counting coup. As a boy, Grandpa and his friends rode into a Comanche camp and stole their ponies. In the ensuing skirmish, Grandpa was severely injured but did not fall off his horse, gaining the warrior name that serves as the book's title.

Initiating Activities

1. Ask students what they know about Oklahoma Territory in the 1890s. Use a variety of maps to help students develop some ideas about the terrain and climate. Point out that Oklahoma did not become a state until 1907 and that in addition to Native American groups who had originally lived there, others had been relocated there from the Southeast. Anglo settlers had only started coming to Oklahoma in 1889, as a result of land giveaways, but their numbers were growing rapidly.

2. Point out the title of the book and the cover illustration. Encourage students to speculate on the significance of the title. Turn to the title page of the book and point out the horses and tepees—both features of the Plains Indians lifestyle.

3. Go over the "Glossary" with students, encouraging them to look for these words in the text and illustrations.

Discussion Questions

1. Why did Saygee say her Grandpa was like a "living book"? Do you know anyone who is a "living book"?

2. According to Grandpa, how is coup like a game of tag? Do you think this is a good comparison? Why or why not?

3. How did Saygee feel when she heard her Grandpa had stolen horses? How did he explain why he had done so? Do you think he would still steal horses at the time he told the story? Why or why not?

4. How did boys spend their time in Oklahoma in the 1890s? Did they have a good reason for deciding to raid the Comanche camp? Explain your answer.

5. Describe what happened on the raid. How did nature help the Kiowa boys? How did nature pose dangers for them?

6. What did the elders tell the young boys about the raid? What do you think the boys learned from the experience?

7. Why did Grandpa get the name Doesn't Fall Off His Horse? Do you think it was a good name for him? Why or why not?

Follow-up Activities

1. Ask students to study the book's colorful illustrations for more clues to the lifestyle of the Kiowa. What technologies did they use? What animals seemed to be important to them? How did geography affect them? Based on the information gathered, have students create brief written descriptions of life in a Kiowa camp.

2. Encourage students to develop a hypothesis about why the horse and tepee were features of life among the Plains Indians. (They were nomadic people who moved often, following the buffalo, and thus needed portable homes and a means of transportation.) Make resources available that will allow students to compare forms of housing used by Native Americans in several regions—the Northeast, Great Plains, and Southwest, for example. Why was each well-suited to the environment and/or lifestyle of the group who used it? A useful book is *First Houses: Native American Homes and Sacred Structures*, by Jean Guard Monroe and Ray A. Williamson, illustrated by Susan Johnston Carlson (Boston: Houghton Mifflin, 1993), which provides a wealth of information about Native American architecture.

3. Ask interested students to do the research needed to create a timeline showing the events that Grandpa had seen in his lifetime. Other students could illustrate the timeline using Virginia Stroud's bright style.

Family Pictures/Cuadros de familia,
written and illustrated by Carmen Lomas Garza (San Francisco, CA: Children's Book Press, 1990).

Summary

The vignettes in this book, written in both English and Spanish, describe the action in the author/illustrator's paintings of family life when she was growing up in Kingsville, Texas. Among the activities she portrays are a trip to a fair across the border in Mexico, a birthday party with traditional piñata, picking cactus, going to church, and sitting on the porch on a warm summer evening.

Initiating Activities

1. Tell students that they are going to be reading a book called *Family Pictures*. Ask them to suggest things that might be in a book with that title.

2. Show students the book and point out the second title, *Cuadros de familia*. What do they think this means? What does it suggest about the family that is written about in the book?

3. Read aloud the author's explanation of the book. Depending on your class, you may choose to read in English, Spanish, or both. Help students find Kingsville, Texas, on a map of the United States and make some hypotheses about what living in Kingsville would be like. Focus particularly on the likely weather and physical surroundings.

Discussion Questions

1. What were some of the things Carmen saw at the fair in Reynosa? Use both the words and picture in answering the question. Have you ever been to a street fair? How was the fair you attended different from this Mexican fair held when Carmen was a girl?

2. When do you think Carmen grew up—the 1940s, 1950s, 1960s, or 1970s? What evidence can you find in the story or pictures?

3. When Carmen and her brothers and sisters visited their grandparents, many of the activities seemed to be related to food. Were any of these activities surprising to you? Why? Do you think you would have known more about these activities if you grew up in an area with the same climate and plant life as Kingsville, Texas? Do you think you would have known more about these activities if you grew up in a small town? Or if you grew up around the same time as Carmen did?

4. List some of the traditions Carmen describes that are part of Hispanic culture. Which of these traditions are still popular today? Which are popular outside Hispanic culture? Why do you think other groups have borrowed these traditions?

5. What do you think the author meant when she said that her mother "also laid out the bed for our dreams of the future"? How do you think her mother did that? How do you think her mother feels about Carmen's success as an artist? Has anyone helped you lay out the bed for your dreams of the future?

6. Pick the picture and story that you like best. Explain why you like it. What do the picture and story tell you about Carmen's family history? Why do you think Carmen chose to draw this picture and write this story? Why were they important to her?

Follow-up Activities

1. Ask students to create picture books showing and explaining their own family history. Students may choose events that parallel those described in the book or may select events that are especially important to them. If students or their parents are bilingual, encourage them to present the text in both English and their family's first language. When they complete their books, ask them to reflect on how their experiences are similar to and different from Carmen's. What are the main reasons for the similarities? What are the main reasons for the differences? Students should consider ethnic background, geographic area, rural/suburban/urban factors, and time period.

2. Encourage students to research some of the traditions mentioned in the book. How did foods like tacos and tamales develop? How have they been spread to other areas? Is the cakewalk a Hispanic tradition, or was it borrowed from another culture? What is the history of the piñata? How are piñatas made? The book, *The Piñata Maker: El Piñatero*, by George Ancona (San Diego: Harcourt Brace, 1994; primary) could be a useful resource in pursuing the questions related to piñatas.

Dinner at Aunt Connie's House,
written and illustrated by Faith Ringgold
(New York: Hyperion Books, 1993).

Summary

Nine-year-old Melody goes with her family to Aunt Connie's house, where she meets her new adopted cousin, Lonnie. Together, the children discover 12 portraits of eminent African-American women from history. Amazingly, the portraits can speak, telling the youngsters of their work and experiences, providing a powerful example of how art can inspire us.

Initiating Activities

1. Share with students the title of the book they are about to read. How many of them have visited an aunt's house? What kinds of things did they do? Did they have fun? What other relatives do they see when they visit their aunt?

2. Next, show students the cover of the book. What seems unusual about this dinner? (Two children are sitting at the table with 12 paintings.) Based on this picture, what do the students think might happen at Aunt Connie's house? Read the dedication page to students. Does it give students any additional ideas about the book?

Discussion Questions

1. Why did Aunt Connie and Uncle Bates invite the family to dinner every summer? When your family gets together, do they share art, music, or stories? If you were going to share a talent with your relatives, what would it be?

2. What did Melody find so unusual about Lonnie? Do you find this unusual? Why or why not?

3. Were you surprised that the paintings could speak? Could this happen in real life? In what ways might a painting be able to "speak"?

4. What do you think it meant when the painting of Rosa Parks said, "Your aunt Connie created us to tell you the history of our struggle"? What struggle was she talking about? Do you think paintings are a good way to tell about history? Have you learned about any other historical events by looking at paintings? What other ways could someone use to tell about African Americans' struggle for equal rights?

5. How many of the women in the portraits did you know about before reading this book? Which ones did you find most interesting? Did any of the women's stories make you sad? angry? Why? Which women do you think changed other people's lives the most?

6. Do you think it was important for Lonnie and Melody to know about the women in the paintings? Do you think it is important for you and other students to know about them? Explain your answer.

Follow-up Activities

1. Help the students construct a timeline on butcher paper. Put the line and dates in the center of the paper, so that people and events can be added above and below the line. Above the line, have students show the women whose lives are described in the book. Encourage them to add more people to the timeline, perhaps expanding to include people from other groups who have struggled for equal rights. Challenge students to use the space below the line to show events that were occurring in the United States while the people they have shown above the line were living. Encourage them to show events that were influenced by the people, as well as events that may have influenced them. To connect with the book's view that art speaks to us, the timeline should be illustrated.

2. Organize the students into pairs or trios and assign each one of the women from the portraits. Students should try to find two additional types of sources about the person; these might include a biography, a speech given by the person, a song or play about the person, something written by the person, an artifact that would represent the person's life or work, or a photograph of the person. If you think that it will be difficult for students to find materials on all the women, you may want to focus on those on whom material is more readily available, such as Rosa Parks and Harriet Tubman. Arrange for all the groups to display their materials on the same day; structure time so that students can examine the materials collected by other groups. Conduct a discussion of which sources students prefer. Which provide the most information? Which are easiest to use? Which do students think are most accurate? Encourage students to continue looking for many kinds of sources as they study history.

3. Read portions of the background material that the author has provided at the end of the book, especially the last paragraph, in which she describes her views of art. Discuss this statement with students; then challenge students to create a work of art that illustrates proud events in the life of someone they think made a difference in history. Create a "Talking Art" wall where the work can be displayed for your class and, if feasible, others.

Summary

In this charming story, neighbors of all ages sit on Miss Ida's porch and share stories. On this particular night, elders recount stories of brushes with history, including a visit by Duke Ellington's orchestra and Marian Anderson's concert at the Lincoln Memorial. The narrator of the story is a young girl who finds security in the sharing and pride in the stories told.

Initiating Activities

1. Ask students if their home has a porch. Most students' homes probably will not. Draw a home with porch on the chalkboard or show the book's cover illustration. Ask students to speculate on what kinds of activities would occur on a porch in the evening. Read the dedication of the book to the class. What kind of activities does the author think should take place on porches? Why does the author think these activities are important?

2. If possible, play a recording of Duke Ellington's or Marian Anderson's music to the class. Ask students what they think of the music. (If you cannot find recordings by either of these artists, you might play selections by contemporary African-American jazz or opera artists, such as Wynton Marsalis, Herbie Hancock, Bobby McFerrin, and Jessye Norman.) Can they imagine a time when great performers such as Ellington and Anderson would not be allowed to play or stay in certain places? Tell students they will hear about such a time in this story.

Discussion Questions

1. What does the narrator of the story call the very best time of the day? Why is this a special time? What time of the day do you think is the very best? Why?

2. What is an in-between kid? How are their activities different from those of the little kids and the big kids? Are you an in-between kid? Why or why not?

3. How did Mr. Fisher meet Duke Ellington? Even though this was a good memory, it also made Mr. Fisher angry. Why? How does Mr. Fisher's story make you feel?

4. What story did Shoo Kate share? Why did her father cry with pride and sadness at the Marian Anderson concert? Have you ever experienced pride and sadness at the same time? When?

5. What kind of a man was Uncle Henry? Why did Uncle Henry think that knowledge of history was the most important story children could ever be told? Do you agree? What stories about your history have fueled your mind?

6. Where did Uncle Henry take his nieces and nephews? What was so exciting about this event? Why do you think Uncle Henry said "You can know where you are going in this world only if you know where you've been"?

Follow-up Activities

1. Read the concluding note from the author and encourage students to read more about Duke Ellington and Marian Anderson. Students who do so may want to create posters and present dramatizations about the lives of these two great musicians.

2. With the class, investigate in more depth the events surrounding Marian Anderson's banning from Constitution Hall. Constitution Hall belonged to the Daughters of the American Revolution, a group of women whose ancestors had fought in the American Revolution. Eleanor Roosevelt was a member of this group. When the DAR refused to let Marian Anderson sing at Constitution Hall, Mrs. Roosevelt resigned from the organization. Distribute Handout 1 to the class and read it with students. Do they think the letter states Mrs. Roosevelt's position strongly enough? Why or why not? What might the political consequences of this action be? Many analysts believe that Mrs. Roosevelt's position helped her husband win reelection in 1940, because it strengthened support for FDR among African-Americans and white liberals in the north.

3. Organize "An Evening on the Porch," in which you invite older members of your community to visit with your students, sharing stories about your community or about encounters with either famous people or historical events.

Eleanor Roosevelt Resigns from the DAR

February 26, 1939

My dear Mrs. Robert:

I am afraid that I have never been a very useful member of the Daughters of the American Revolution, so I know it will make very little difference to you whether I resign, or whether I continue to be a member of your organization.

However, I am in complete disagreement with the attitude taken in refusing Constitution Hall to a great artist. You have set an example which seems to me unfortunate, and I feel obliged to send in to you my resignation. You had an opportunity to lead in an enlightened way and it seems to me that your organization has failed.

I realize that many people will not agree with me, but feeling as I do this seems to me the only proper procedure to follow.

Very sincerely yours

Christmas in the Big House, Christmas in the Quarters,
by Patricia C. McKissack and Frederick L. McKissack, illustrated by John Thompson (New York: Scholastic, 1994).

Summary

Christmas festivities among plantation owners and slaves in 1859 Tidewater Virginia are detailed in this beautifully illustrated book. While both groups enjoyed special holiday traditions, potential political changes could not be completely ignored, as whites worried about such events as John Brown's raid on Harper's Ferry and blacks shared news from smuggled-in abolitionist newspapers.

Initiating Activities

1. Ask students to think of a holiday or other event celebrated in their families. Have them jot down traditions associated with the celebration. Next, have them circle the traditions they think might be practiced by a family in different circumstances from their own—richer, poorer, having a different cultural background, living in a different country or a different part of the United States. What accounts for the similarities? (Shared history, similar beliefs) What accounts for the differences? (Different family/regional/etc. experiences, resources)

2. Share with students the "Authors' Note" at the beginning of the book. When is this book set? What is special about this time period? Where is the book set? Be sure students understand what is meant by "Big House" and "Quarters." Have students speculate about differences and similarities between Christmas celebrations in the Big House and the Quarters. Be sure students are aware of the "Notes" section at the end of the book before they begin reading.

Discussion Questions

1. What is similar about reactions to the first frost among children in the Big House and those in the Quarters? What beliefs and experiences help explain the similarities? What experiences explain differences in their reactions and the answers parents give to their children's questions?

2. What preparations for Christmas take place in the Big House and in the Quarters? Imagine that you are a slave woman preparing for Christmas. What feelings might you be experiencing? Script a conversation between two slave women as they sit sewing in the Quarters late at night.

3. What does the young servant hear the master's family talking about on the day of the tree-trimming? Why were these events important to the family? Why were they also important to the people in the Quarters? How did the two groups see these events differently?

4. Make a Christmas Eve schedule for a boy who lives in the Big House and one who lives in the Quarters. What are the similarities and differences?

5. Why do you think some slaves refused to join the master's family on Christmas Eve? What do you think you would do in a similar situation?

6. Describe the role of stories and songs in preparing for and celebrating Christmas in the Quarters and the Big House. Why were songs and stories important? Give examples to support your reasons.

7. Describe the gifts exchanged between slaves and the master's family. What do you think the authors mean when they say gifts were "graciously given and humbly received" or "humbly given and graciously received"? Who is humble? Who is gracious? Could these roles be reversed? Why or why not?

8. What do you think the quote from Dickens means? Does it "contain the seeds of rebellion," as one of the older men complains?

9. Why do the master and his wife visit the Quarters on Christmas night? What evidence can you find in the book that the slaves aren't "happy"? Explain how the quotation below relates to your answer: "Maybe if we sing loud enough they won't hear us crying."

10. List some of the traditions or superstitions associated with New Year's Day. Do you know of any of these traditions or superstitions still practiced or talked about today?

11. What happened at noon on New Year's Day? Does knowing about this event change your thinking about the Christmas celebrations? Why or why not?

12. List the different ways information is conveyed in the book (e.g., illustrations, text, song lyrics, recipes, menus). Why do you think the authors included so many different sources? Which are most interesting to you? most informative? most accurate? Explain your answers.

Follow-up Activities

1. Assign students to make an illustrated timeline of the events referred to by whites and blacks in the book and/or to make posters describing the lives of famous people who are mentioned.

2. Point out that the authors chose a 20th-century poem by Langston Hughes to illustrate one of the book's important ideas—that laughter and celebration can hide deep pain. Encourage students to create their own ways of expressing this idea, either artistically (through a song, poem, painting, or dance) or through a story or essay in which they give other historical examples of this idea.

3. Have students list all the functions that music played in the story—for worship, to make work go faster, to express deep feelings, to communicate a coded message to someone, to accompany dancing, etc. For each function on their list, encourage students to think of contemporary and historical examples of music's use in the same way. A number of books

about African-American music are available for students who want to learn more about music's role in one cultural community. Some possibilities include *All Day, All Night*, selected and illustrated by Ashley Bryan (New York: Atheneum, 1991), a collection of 20 spirituals; *What a Morning*, selected by John Langstaff, illustrated by Ashley Bryan (New York: Macmillan, 1987), a collection of five spirituals that tell the Christmas story; *Follow the Drinking Gourd*, by Jeannete Winter (New York: Knopf, 1988), which tells of one slave family's flight to freedom following the directions provided in a song's lyrics; and *Black Music in America: A History through Its People*, by James Haskins (New York: Crowell, 1987).

Guests,
by Michael Dorris
(New York: Hyperion Books, 1994).

Summary

In this book, Michael Dorris tells the story of an event similar to the first Thanksgiving, but initiated by the Native Americans when their harvest is bountiful and the new settlers are hungry. The central character is a boy named Moss, who is unhappy about the guests he believes will spoil the harvest feast. Angry with his parents, he runs into the woods where he confronts several truths about himself and growing up.

Initiating Activities

1. Tell students the title of the book they will be reading. Ask them how they feel when they are going to have guests. How is the situation different when they know the guests well as opposed to when they do not know the guests? What if the guests did not speak the same language as the students and their families? Encourage students to share their thoughts about these questions.

2. Explain to students that the author does not specifically say where or when the story takes place. Direct them to look for clues as to the setting as they read the story.

Discussion Questions

(for use after reading chapters 1 and 2)

1. What is wampum? How did people in the story use wampum? What did Moss's grandfather say about remaking the broken wampum belt? How did Moss feel about "losing the story"? How might one of your family's stories be lost? (For example, photographs that remind family members of a particular story could be lost or destroyed.)

2. What is away time? Why is Moss so curious about it? Would you have the same feelings if you were going to experience something like away time?

3. Describe the argument that Moss was having with his father and mother about the guests. With whom do you agree? Why? Pick a quotation from one of these three characters that best summarizes your view on the guests.

4. What did Moss mean when he said the feast "was the echo of something that had happened and happened and happened"? Why was this important to him? Can you think of an occasion that reminds you of things that have "happened and happened and happened" in your family's life? Explain how the two events are similar and different.

5. How did Moss's grandmother explain why Moss and Trouble were given those names? Can you think of people you know whose nicknames reflect the same naming principles?

How might having a name like Trouble make a person feel about themselves? Explain your answer.

6. Why did Moss walk into the forest? List as many reasons as you can. Do you think Moss made a good decision? Why or why not?

(for use after reading chapters 3 and 4)

7. Describe Moss's experiences in the forest. Which would you classify as "good" experiences? Which would you call "bad" experiences. How did you decide?

8. What did Moss realize about himself when he was talking to the porcupine? Do you agree that he was "not very nice"? Give examples from the story to support your answer.

9. Moss remembered a conversation in which he and his mother talked about what made something beautiful. How did his thinking about what was beautiful change in the forest? Have you ever changed your mind about whether something was beautiful when you saw it in a new way?

10. Why does Trouble want to be a boy? Make a list of things that girls and boys did in Trouble and Moss's culture. What things are on both lists? What things have to do with being young? What things still apply today?

(for use after reading chapters 5 and 6)

11. Describe the story of Running Woman. Why was this story so important to Trouble? What did Moss think of the story? Whose view of the story is more like your own?

12. Why did Moss think he had spent more time in the forest than he actually had? Have you ever had an experience like this, when you lost track of time? Describe that experience.

13. What did Moss realize about his father when he returned to their home? If Moss's father didn't really want the guests to attend the feast, why do you think he invited them?

(for use after reading chapters 7 and 8)

14. Describe the story "How the People Lost Each Other." What is the meaning of this story? Does it have a "moral"? If so, what do you think the moral is? Why was this a good or bad story to tell the guests?

15. What did Trouble mean when she said "I can't be what they want"? What do you think her family wanted her to be?

16. What did the guests do that shocked Moss and his grandfather? Is this an example of what happens when two groups have different customs and cannot communicate about them?

17. Describe the story of "The Beaver and the Muskrat Woman." Why do you think Moss's mother chose to tell this story? Why did it sound different to Moss than it had other times he had heard it? Do you think our own stories change as our lives change?

18. Two times in the story, characters mention being invisible. What do you think it means to be invisible to other people? Is being invisible a good feeling? Why or why not?

6. Who was Howard Crow? Why were Julie and Daniel excited about Howard Crow?

(for use after reading the third, fourth, and fifth chapters)

7. Why do you think Julie said "nothing bad could ever happen to me and Daniel"? From what you have read so far, was she right? Is there anyone that makes you feel "unmovable, strong, eternal" when you are with them?

8. What was a dinosaur prospector? How did they go about doing their work? What kind of tools did they use? Why did Jim and Brett think that the prospector named Hump was a "filthy rotten snake"? Do you agree?

9. Why was it so important to Julie when Daniel said he was a farmer?

10. Describe what happened when Julie and Daniel found the dinosaur bones. What did they do? How did they feel?

(for use after reading the sixth, seventh, and eighth chapters)

11. Why was getting the letter sent to Howard Crow so complicated? How would the process of informing Howard Crow be different today? What accounts for the changes in communications?

12. Describe Hump Hinton and his wife. Which is a more interesting character? Why?

13. Reread the dinosaur poem. Do you think it is a good description of dinosaur skeletons you have seen in museums? Write a poem of your own describing a dinosaur skeleton.

(for use after reading the ninth, tenth, and eleventh chapters)

14. How did Daniel keep Hump from finding his dinosaur? What did Grandma compare this strategy to?

15. How did Daniel die? How does the description of Daniel's death make you feel? Write a letter to Julie, expressing your feelings about her brother's death.

16. Why did Jarvis and Julie take one of the bones from the dinosaur? Do you think this was a good idea? Why or why not?

(for use after reading the twelfth, thirteenth, and fourteenth chapters)

17. What happened to Hump Hinton? Why do you think Amba did what she did?

18. How did Julie feel when Howard Crow came to get the dinosaur? How did she feel when she found out how much money Crow would pay for the dinosaur? Why did she eventually decide that it was all right for Daniel's dinosaur to go with Howard Crow? Do you agree with her?

Follow-up Activities

1. Follow reading and discussion of the book with a trip to a natural history museum, giving students a special assignment to pay attention to information about where skeletal remains of dinosaurs were found. In what states were they found? Does the museum indi-

cate whether they were found in fields, streambeds, etc.? Encourage students to create a map or chart that shows the information they have gathered.

2. Julie and Daniel had a very close relationship. Have students look for other examples of close sibling relationships in books. What are some of the traits that the pairs they find have in common? What are the benefits of such a close relationship? Does it seem to matter when or where close siblings lived? Encourage students to write poems or essays that reflect their thinking about siblings in literature.

3. Remind students that the author said that some of what was in the book was "lies." Encourage them to use other sources to verify or disprove historical information in the story.

Dear Levi:
Letters from the Overland Trail,
by Elvira Woodruff, illustrated by Beth Peck
(New York: Alfred A. Knopf, 1994).

Summary

This novel is presented as a series of letters from 12-year-old Austin to his younger brother, Levi. When the boys' father died in Oregon and their mother died back home in Pennsylvania, Austin decided to travel west to check on their father's land claim. His journey along the Overland Trail, which he documents in his letters, is marked by adventure, tragedy, and hard work. When he arrives in Oregon, all is not as he had anticipated either, but with the help of a friend, he is able to lay the foundation for his own and his brother's future.

Initiating Activities

1. Share with students the title of the book and the cover illustration. Using these two pieces of information, what do they think the book is about? What might be special about the way in which it is written?

2. Read the "Preface" aloud with students and allow them to speculate on the significance of the letters and the button book. Do they know what a button book is? If not, what do they think it might be?

3. Next, show students the map of the Overland Trail on the next two pages of the book. What do students know or what can they infer from the map about the land that the trail covers? What kinds of obstacles or adventures might people encounter traveling the Overland Trail in 1851? If possible, post a large map of the United States—either a physical map or a political map of the United States in 1851—in the classroom so that students can follow Austin's journey from Pennsylvania to Oregon.

Discussion Questions

(for use after reading Austin's April letters)

1. Make a schedule showing the events in Austin's day. Then make a schedule showing the events in your own day. Are there any similarities? What are the most glaring differences? Do you think you would do well on Austin's schedule? Do you think he would do well on yours?

2. What combination of events resulted in Austin's traveling to Oregon with the Morrison family rather than members of his own family?

3. Pick one of the people traveling with Austin and draw a picture of that person complete with a "cartoon bubble" showing something they might be saying. Explain to your classmates how you decided what the person would look like and what they might be saying.

4. What aspect of the weather was a problem for the wagon train in Ohio and Indiana? What problems did it cause? Study any maps you can find that would help you decide whether you could plot a route to Oregon that would avoid this problem.

5. Compare the medical and dental practices available on the wagon train to your own experiences with doctors and dentists. What specific changes or developments that we have today would have helped Austin and his friends? Would any of the practices of 1851 be useful today? Explain your answer.

6. What is the significance of Mrs. Morrison's rocking chair? What did it make Austin remember? Have you ever had the experience of suddenly remembering something that you had not thought of in a long time? What was that experience like?

(for use after reading Austin's May letters)

7. Who is Reuben McAlister Rice? Why is he so special to Austin and his friends? Do you think Reuben will be an important person in the story? What evidence suggests that he will be?

8. Why were buttons so important to Reuben? How did Austin, Frank, and Hiram react to the buttons and their chance to trade buttons with Reuben? Do you have any possessions you keep to remind you of someone you once knew? What would a button that reminded someone of you be made of? What would it look like?

9. Why does Mr. Morrison love maps? Do you agree that maps "give a man room to wander"?

10. Describe the argument that Mr. Morrison and Mr. Hickman had about Indians. What does Austin think about the disagreement? Do you agree with Austin? Why or why not?

(for use after reading Austin's June letters)

11. What events was Austin referring to when he said he wished he "never lived to see what I had to see today"? Why does the sound of the Indian man's cry stay with Austin? Have you ever heard a sound so sad that it is hard to forget?

12. Do you agree with Reuben that "a person who never sees any good in others is very likely not to have many good qualities himself"? Give examples from this book and others to support your position.

13. What did the Morrisons tell Austin that made him happy? Use quotes from the book to explain why you think Mr. Morrison is or is not a hero.

14. Mr. Hickman tried to say Mr. Morrison's death was Frank's fault. Do you agree? Make a list of all the events or factors that contributed to Mr. Morrison's death. After examining the list, can you determine whether one person or event was "responsible" for Mr. Morrison's death. Try to make a case for Mr. Morrison's death being the responsibility of the Indian who killed him, Frank, Mr. Hickman, Mr. Morrison himself (for deciding to travel to the West, which was the Indian's home).

15. What did the militia do to allow the train to continue? Make a list of reasons for and against the militia's actions. Which reasons are most convincing? Which characters in the book would agree with your reasoning?

16. Why wasn't Reuben pleased when Mr. Hart's men killed two buffalo? Do you think the people on the wagon train made good use of the buffalo? Why or why not?

(for use after reading Austin's July and August letters)

17. How has the terrain being covered by the wagon train changed from April to July? What problems does the geographic location cause for the wagon train at the end of June? Could these problems have been avoided? Again, consult a map to see if a better route could have been taken.

18. What evidence do Austin's letters give that he is beginning to get tired and discouraged? What events helped encourage him? What events made him feel worse?

19. What did Reuben and Austin do with Mrs. Morrison's rocking chair after she died? How did this make Austin feel? How does it make you feel reading about it?

20. Describe some of the foods Austin has eaten—or been offered—on the trip. Are there any that you think 12-year-olds today would still enjoy? Are there any you think 12-year-olds today would refuse to eat?

21. Describe the prank that Austin and his friends played on the Judson brothers. What do you think this prank might show about similarities and differences between young people in 1851 and young people in the 1990s?

(for use after reading Austin's September letters)

22. Describe the surroundings in Oregon. What ways of living would the settlers be able to pursue there?

23. Describe what happened at the lumber camp. Were you surprised by Mr. Zikes's actions? Were you surprised by Reuben's actions?

24. Predict what you think will be happening one year from Austin's last letter. Do you think Levi will be in Oregon? Why or why not?

Follow-up Activities

1. Ask each student to pick a favorite quotation from Reuben and create a drawing, mobile, poster, or other work illustrating what the quotation means. Encourage them to think about the quotation in the context of both the story and applications to their own lives.

2. Direct students' attention to the map on which they tracked the wagon train's progress. Remind them of the thinking they did about other possible routes West. Ask students to predict the routes of trails going from the east to the present-day locations of San Francisco and Los Angeles. Then have them find maps showing the Old Spanish Trail, Santa Fe Trail, Mormon Trail, and California Trail to evaluate the accuracy of their predictions. What hardships might travelers on each of these trails have experienced because of the natural environment?

Steal Away Home,
by Lois Ruby
(New York: Macmillan, 1994).

Summary

Through alternating stories set in Lawrence, Kansas—in 1856 and the present—Lois Ruby helps young people better understand events prior to the Civil War, as well as the excitement of uncovering historic information. When Dana and her family move into a historic house, they find a skeleton and diary in a small, boarded-up alcove. Through Dana's reading of the diary and the alternating story of the Quaker family that lived in the house in the 1850s, readers learn about the courage and wisdom of a young black woman named Lizbet Charles, who helped slaves escape to freedom along the Underground Railroad.

Initiating Activities

1. Ask students what they would do if they found a skeleton hidden behind a wall in their house. What would they want to know about the person whose remains these were? How might they go about finding out about the person? Tell students that the book they are going to be reading deals with just such a situation.

2. Read the John Steinbeck quotation that serves as the epigraph for the book. What do students think the quotation means? What does it suggest about the author's thinking?

Discussion Questions

(for use after reading chapters 1-5)

1. What four items were in the small room behind the wall that Dana discovered? What hypotheses, if any, can you make about the room based on these items and the fact that the room was a closed off part of a larger room?

2. Who are the members of the Weaver family? How long have they been in Lawrence? Why was James so scared, living in Lawrence?

3. What "visitors" came to stay with the Weavers? Where had they come from? Where were they going? How did they know the Weavers' house was a safe place to stay?

4. What was Dr. Baxi's working hypothesis about the skeleton after he conducted the autopsy? What evidence did he have to support his hypothesis? What would you recommend that Dana do next in trying to determine whether Dr. Baxi's hypothesis was correct?

5. Describe the conflict between the Free Soilers and the proslavery forces in 1856 Kansas. How did the location of Kansas influence the conflict? How did the conflict affect where people settled?

6. Describe how Mr. and Mrs. Weaver were doing their part to end slavery in different ways. Given that Mr. Weaver was also against slavery, why do you think Mrs. Weaver wanted to keep the fugitive slaves a secret? Do you think this was a good decision? Why or why not?

7. How did being Quakers influence the Weavers? Why did being a Quaker sometimes frustrate James?

(for use after reading chapters 6-12)

8. After Mr. Weaver returned, what did you learn about why Mrs. Weaver didn't tell Mr. Weaver about the slaves? Who do you think was right—Mr. Weaver or Mrs. Weaver? Explain your answer. Can you think of other examples in U.S. history when people disagreed about whether a bad law should be obeyed or not?

9. What was Ahn referring to when she said, "Such a thing, even in this country"? Why might the information in the diary have affected Ahn and Dana somewhat differently?

10. Describe the events that led up to the burning of Lawrence. Do you think these events could be called a "little civil war? Why or why not?

11. James was "scared he'd get hurt, and scared he'd run. Scared he'd bloody someone...and scared he'd kill someone, and scared he'd be glad he did it." Explain what you think this quotation means.

12. How was Lizbet Charles different from other fugitives who stayed with the Weavers? What problems did Lizbet's presence pose for Mrs. Weaver? What do you think she should do?

(for use after reading chapters 13-18)

13. What kinds of stories does Lizbet tell the Weavers? Why do you think these stories are important to her? Why do you think she chooses to tell them to the Weavers?

14. Why did Dana decide to let Jeep read the diary? How did Jeep react to the stories written there? What comparison did Dana make with Martin Luther King? Do you think it was a good analogy? Why or why not?

15. What happened to Solomon? If you were Mr. Weaver, would these events change your ideas about upholding the Fugitive Slave Law? Explain your answer. Write what you think Mr. Weaver should say to officials in Missouri when he tries to get Solomon back.

16. What were some of the remedies Lizbet knew? Do you think the indigo root tea cured Rebecca? Do you think spreading manure on his face would remove James's freckles? On what grounds are you deciding whether you think the remedies would work?

17. What happened to Matthew Luke Charles? How did this influence his wife, Lizbet? What would you have done in Lizbet's place? Can you think of any modern-day examples of people who have been spurred on by a spouse's murder?

(for use after reading chapters 19-24)

18. What evidence have you seen that James might be a good architect? Sketch the kind of building that James imagined. Do you think this style of building would be well suited to a prairie environment? Why or why not?

19. List natural and human obstacles Lizbet faced on her trips back to rescue slaves. Use evidence from the book and maps of Kansas and Missouri to develop your list.

20. Why did Bethany Maxwell's family decide to move to Oregon? If you had lived in Kansas in 1856, would you have wanted to stay or leave? Why?

21. Explain the origins of the term *hush puppies* as described by Jeep. Try to verify or disprove this explanation.

22. Why was James so upset about what he "ought" to have said to Will before he left? How would you answer the question: "What do you say to a violent man about nonviolence?" Does Mr. Weaver's story help you answer the question? How did you think James will answer the question for himself?

(for use after reading chapters 25-31)

23. Do you think James was right in saying that not telling their father about Lizbet was "lying"? Why do you think Mrs. Weaver said it wasn't "lying, exactly"? Write a diary entry for James, explaining his feelings about this "lying."

24. Did what Dr. Baxi learned from scientific tests match what Dana learned from the diary? What you have learned from the stories from 1856 that you have read? How did scientific evidence and historical information combine to provide a good, but incomplete description of what happened to Lizbet? Can our reconstruction of the past ever be complete? Why or why not?

25. What happened when Mr. Weaver finally met Lizbet Charles? Were you surprised by his reaction? Why or why not?

26. Why was Dana so intent on going into the Wolcott Castle? In Dana's place, would you have gone into the castle despite your father's warnings? What did she, Ahn, and Jeep find in the tower that linked the castle to James's experiences as a teenager? Why does she say "What a guy" when she thinks about James?

27. Why was Lizbet Charles in the walled-in area of the room upstairs in Dana's house?

28. In what ways were James and his family similar to Dana and her family? In what ways were they different? What accounts for the similarities and differences?

Follow-up Activities

1. The stories Lizbet Charles told about dramatic escapes from slavery are among those told in *Escape from Slavery: Five Journeys to Freedom*, by Doreen Rappaport, illustrated by Charles Lilly (New York: HarperCollins, 1991; intermediate, advanced). Based on newspaper stories of the time and accounts written by people involved with the Underground Railroad, the book dramatically tells of five daring escapes. The stories in this book could be compared with the stories told by Lizbet. To involve students further in the stories told in *Escape from Slavery*, divide the class into five groups, assigning each group one of the stories to present to the class through a simulated press conference with the people in-

volved. Make a map available so that the escaped slaves can show where they started their journey, how they traveled, and where they finally settled.

2. Encourage students to write a diary entry for someone who might have lived in their house (or on the location of their house) in the 1850s. Would any experiences be similar to those of Mrs. Weaver? Why or why not?

3. Older students could compare *Steal Away Home* with *Journey of the Sparrows*, by Fran Leeper Buss, with the assistance of Daisy Cubias (New York: Dell, 1991). This book tells of the struggles of two Salvadoran sisters to get to the United States, survive a Chicago winter while avoiding *la migra*, provide for their brother and a new baby born to the older sister, and send money to their mother and sister, who escaped only as far as Mexico. The efforts to achieve asylum for Salvadorans, led by a local Catholic priest, provide a basis for comparison with the Quakers' role in the Underground Railroad. Similarly, the role of "conductors" on the Underground Railroad (e.g., Lizbet Charles and Harriet Tubman), who helped others escape for altruistic reasons, could be compared with the role of *coyotes*, who seem to be motivated primarily by the hope of financial gain.

White Lilacs,
by Carolyn Meyer
(Orlando, FL: Harcourt Brace, 1993).

Summary

Based on a historical incident, this book recounts the struggle to survive of a black community in Texas when their white neighbors decide to take black families' land for a city park. The central character is 12-year-old Rose Lee Jefferson, who hears about the plans for the park as she serves meals at a white family's home. Rose Lee's own relatives react in different ways to the threatened relocation, often with unanticipated results.

Initiating Activities

1. Show students a picture of a lilac and ask them if they are familiar with this flower. Explain that while purple lilacs are common in some parts of the country, white lilacs are rare. Explain that students will be reading a book entitled *White Lilacs*. Ask students why an author would name a book for a rare flower. Accept all answers.

2. Next, read the title of the book's first chapter and the first sentence of the book aloud. Are students surprised by what this first sentence suggests about the story? Does it match their thinking about the title? How are the first sentence and the title linked? Do students think gardening will somehow play an important part in this story? What kinds of things are associated with a garden? How might that be important to the story?

Discussion Questions

(for use after reading chapters 1-4)

1. For Rose Lee, what event is associated with the white lilac being in bloom? Suggest two reasons why this event was so important in Rose Lee's life.

2. How was Rose Lee's neighborhood different from the part of town in which the Bells lived? What did Rose Lee love about her neighborhood? Consider places, memories, and people.

3. What was Rose Lee's "special gift"? Do you think she will have the opportunity to take art lessons from Miss Emily Firth? What does the author say to lead you to that conclusion?

4. How were the white people of Dillon planning to take the black people's homes for the park? Why couldn't the black people stop them from doing so? How did members of Rose Lee's family and their friends and neighbors react to this plan? Which person do you think you would have agreed with if you lived in Freedomtown in 1921?

(for use after reading chapters 5-8)

5. Why hadn't Rose Lee and Catherine Jane "had a good talk for a long time"? When they finally did talk, what did they talk about? How did Rose Lee feel about their conversation? Do you think their friendship will continue as they get older? Why or why not?

6. What did Rose Lee hear at the Bells' dinner party that upset her? Why did she feel invisible? Have you ever had a similar feeling?

7. When the Jeffersons discuss the election to be held on July 5, Mr. Jefferson mentions that Henry had been in France. Remembering that the story takes place in 1921, why do you think he was in France? Do you think his experience as a soldier in World War I might have influenced his views on the events in Dillon? Why or why not?

8. Why was Rose Lee both proud of Henry and scared for him when he spoke up in church on Juneteenth? Do you think Henry was courageous, foolish, or both? Explain your answer.

(for use after reading chapters 9-12)

9. Describe the march and picnic that occurred on Juneteenth. What options were black families considering if they lost their homes? What would you have wanted your family to do in that situation?

10. How did the whites of Dillon retaliate following the march to the courthouse square on Juneteenth? What do you think the KKK members hoped to accomplish by their actions?

11. What was Juneteenth a celebration of? What is the importance of the two holidays—Juneteenth and the Fourth of July—to the story? How were the two celebrations similar? How were they different? What do you think of Henry's suggestion that all of the black people simply stop working for the whites for one day?

12. What did Miss Emily Firth do at the Fourth of July picnic? Do you think she was courageous, foolish, or both? How were her actions similar to or different from Henry's and Aunt Susannah's on Juneteenth? Who faced the most negative consequences for their actions? Why?

13. What happened to Henry on the Fourth of July? What were the causes of the tarring and feathering? Think about events, actions, and beliefs.

(to be used after reading chapters 13-16)

14. What does Miss Emily Firth tell Rose Lee to do before Freedomtown is gone? Why does Miss Firth think this is important? Do you agree? Can you think of something in your life that you have wanted to record so that you would not forget it? Is the record you made important to you? What evidence does the author provide that Rose Lee's drawings became important to her and to other people in Freedomtown?

15. What happened to the efforts of Freedomtown's black families to find a good location for their new homes? Write a letter to the editor of the Dillon newspaper explaining your feelings about what happened.

16. When she bobbed her hair, Catherine Jane said "I'm grown-up now." Do you think she was grown up? Why or why not? Who do you think was more grown up—Catherine Jane or Rose Lee? Explain your answer.

17. Why did Aunt Susannah decide to stay in Dillon? Do you think her decision was important to her family? Why or why not?

(for use after reading chapters 17-19)

18. How did moving to the Flats affect the Jefferson family's way of earning a living? What other parts of the community changed because of the move? Describe what you think the most important differences were between life in Freedomtown and life in the Flats.

19. What happened to put Henry's life in danger? How do you feel about these events? Does Catherine Jane's part in getting Henry out of Dillon make you feel differently about her? Why or why not?

20. Why do you think Rose Lee's grandfather worked so hard on his garden at their new home in the Flats? Why do you think he asked Rose Lee to take care of the white lilac right before he died? What is the importance of the fact that the white lilac did not do very well in its new surroundings? What does the white lilac stand for or symbolize?

21. Why might black people "have decided it was better to forget" about Freedomtown and what happened to it? Do you think it is sometimes better to forget about past events or that it is always better to remember? Explain your answer.

Follow-up Activities

1. Read the "Note from the Author" with students and discuss their reactions to finding out that the book is based on an actual event. Are they surprised to hear that people were deprived of their homes in this way in the United States? Point out that people today sometimes lose their homes because of construction projects, such as the building of a university campus, a hospital, or a highway. Many people feel that the neighborhoods of minority or poor people are often targeted for such projects. Encourage interested students to research any such event that has happened in your community. Who lived in the neighborhood that was torn down? Where did they go? Were they able to maintain a sense of community after they moved?

2. Juneteenth is still celebrated in many communities. Encourage students to research the ways in which it is celebrated and compare them to the celebration in Freedomtown. How are they alike? different? What are the common themes of the celebrations?

Dragon's Gate,
by Lawrence Yep
(New York: HarperCollins, 1993).

Summary

Otter, a 14-year-old upper class Chinese boy, longed to go to America with his adoptive father and uncle. With knowledge of American technology, they believed they could help free China from the Manchus. Yet when Otter reached America, his expectations were shattered by the true nature of the work on the transcontinental railroad and his relatives' role in that work. His struggle to survive and maintain his dreams are the focus of Yep's book.

Initiating Activities

1. Ask students to brainstorm what they know about events in U.S. history in the 1860s. Post responses on the chalkboard. Next, ask what they know about Chinese history in the same time period. Do they know of any similarities or links between events in the two countries?

2. Read the "Preface" with students. What links or similarities does it suggest? (Both countries had experienced civil war and strife between groups. Turmoil in China caused many Chinese men to leave the country. Problems building the railroad created a need for workers in the United States, where the Chinese immigrants arrived.) What do students think Yep's book is going to be about?

Discussion Questions

(for use after reading Chapters 1-6)

1. What are the two groups of boys in Otter's school? To which group does Otter belong? How does he feel about his family's status?

2. How does Otter's mother see her family's role? What is the "Work" she thinks the family was put on earth to do? How did Otter's mother's own life show that she was a rebel? How do Foxfire and Squeaky, Otter's father, help carry out the Work? Who in U.S. history might you compare Otter's family to?

3. What disagreements among groups of Chinese people become apparent in the first two chapters? With what other country had the Chinese fought two wars? What effect did these wars have on the people of Three Willows Village? What was the "poison spreading through the whole kingdom"?

4. What did Uncle Foxfire think the Chinese should learn from Americans? Why did he believe modern technology was necessary to the Chinese? Do you agree?

5. Why did the U.S. civil war seem strange to Otter? Can you think of a recent event in U.S. history that would seem strange to someone raised in a culture that believes low status is due to evil deeds in a past life? Can you think of an event in another country that Americans might misinterpret because they believe "all men are created equal"?

6. Why did Otter want to go to America? Why did he decide not to go? In his position, what would you have done?

7. What role does the Dragon's Gate play in the story? After reading Chapters 5 and 6, why do you think Laurence Yep gave his book the title, *Dragon's Gate*?

(for use after reading Chapters 6-11)

8. What surprises does Otter have in his first few days in America? What aspects of the natural environment are alien to him and the other Chinese boys? What does he see that first makes him question Uncle Foxfire's ideas? What do you think Otter is feeling and thinking by the time he reaches the camp?

9. Cite evidence that the class to which a Chinese man belonged remained important in America. Did you find this surprising? Why or why not?

10. What grievances did the Chinese workers have? How does Otter react to the way in which his father and Uncle Foxfire talk to the westerners about these problems? What does Foxfire mean when he says Americans are "better in theory than in practice"? Do you agree? Why or why not?

11. In what ways were Squeaky and Foxfire's crew members misfits? Do you think Otter is a misfit, too? Why or why not?

(for use after reading Chapters 12-17)

12. What dangers did the railroad workers face? What human actions and natural conditions contributed to these dangers? How did the workers try to protect themselves against these dangers? Do workers face such dangers today? How are workers protected now?

13. What role does Sean play in the story? Why do you think the author included this character in the book?

14. What is Kilroy's dream? Why do you think Otter was surprised to learn that westerners dream? Have you ever been surprised to find out that people who seem very different from you are actually similar in some ways? How was your own experience similar to and different from Otter's?

15. Why was Packy's music important to Otter's crew? What do their efforts to get Packy a new moon guitar and the loss of his fingers represent to you? What do you think Otter meant when he said, "This mountain kills singing. It kills laughing. It kills everything. Every day we're here, we die a little."

(for use after reading Chapters 18-23)

16. Otter described walking to work in the tunnel like walking into battle. Who or what was he fighting?

17. What caused the explosion that blinded Squeaky? Who would you hold responsible? Why wasn't anyone punished?

18. Why did Otter refuse to go back to work after the explosion? Why didn't the other Chinese workers stand with him? How are these events similar to what happened when Uncle Foxfire tried to find workers killed by the avalanche? Why do you think Uncle Foxfire stood up to Kilroy after the avalanche but not after the explosion?

19. Why does Foxfire tell Otter than he "can never go home"? Do you agree that someone who has lived in two cultures never fits in either one? Why or why not?

(for use after reading Chapters 24-30)

20. Describe the events that led to Uncle Foxfire's death. How did the experience on the mountain make Otter believe he had come to know his "real uncle"? Describe Uncle Foxfire's strengths and weaknesses as you see them. How are Foxfire and Otter alike and different?

21. Why did Otter decide to stay on the mountain when he had a chance to leave? In his position, what would you have done?

22. What inequities did Sean and Otter discover? What action did the workers decide to take? Why do you think the other men agreed to back Otter this time? How did the bosses retaliate against the workers? Can you think of similar cases in other periods of history?

23. Who seemed to feel more satisfaction about the railroad's completion—Sean or Otter? Why do you think this is true?

24. Why do you think Otter wrote "I won't forget" in the dirt? What wouldn't he forget? What was it a promise to do?

Follow-up Activities

1. Make several standard U.S. history textbooks available to students. Have them analyze what the books include about the building of the Transcontinental Railroads. Are the Chinese and Irish workers mentioned? Are any of the prejudices the Chinese workers faced discussed? Are the dangers the workers faced accurately portrayed? Encourage students to revise the textbook descriptions to be more accurate, using information gained from *Dragon's Gate*.

2. Discuss with students what a monument is—a tangible reminder of something or someone notable or great. Assign students to work in pairs or triads to design a monument to the Chinese workers who helped build the Transcontinental Railroad. When groups have finished their work, display them around the room and conduct a class discussion of the characteristics students think make a monument effective.

3. Interested students could do additional research about the events in Chinese history mentioned in the book, as well as developments later in the 19th century. Students could make a timeline, showing events in China juxtaposed with events in the United States. Encourage students to speculate about whether similar connections could be found between events and other pairs of countries (for example, the United States and Ireland, China and Great Britain).

<table>
<tr><td>

A Break with Charity:
A Story About the Salem Witch Trials,
by Ann Rinaldi
(Orlando, FL: Harcourt Brace Jovanovich, 1992).

</td></tr>
</table>

Summary

Through this story, the author presents one explanation for the accusations of witchcraft in Salem in 1692: that a group of young girls, frustrated and bored by Puritan society, dappled with tea-leaf and palm reading and then made accusations of witchcraft to cover their own activities. Rinaldi weaves this explanation into the story of a young girl who is rejected by the girls in the group, knows the accusations are false, but fears retribution if she speaks out. She must grapple with her own fears and superstitions before she can help end the hysteria.

Initiating Activities

1. Ask students what they know about the Salem witch trials and about Puritan life in general at that time (1692). Post their responses on the chalkboard. Do they have a theory about why the Salem witch trials occurred? Tell students there are many possible explanations, none of which is accepted by everyone. Students are going to read a novel in which the author presents her theory about why the witch trials happened. They can evaluate the theory to see how well they think it explains events.

2. Ask students what they think the title *A Break with Charity* means. They should keep possible meanings in mind as they read the book.

Discussion Questions

(for use after reading prologue)

1. What is going to happen in the Salem Meetinghouse as the book begins? How does the person narrating the story feel about this event? What can we tell has happened in the 14 years since the witch trials?

2. Why do you think the people of Salem refer to the accusations and trials as "the recent tragedy"? Can you think of any events that we refer to by such euphemisms?

(for use after reading chapters 1-6)

3. Why was Susanna English standing outside the parsonage? Why did she think the girls in the parsonage rejected her company? Why did Sarah Bibber think Susanna was standing there? How did Susanna react to that idea?

4. What kind of man was Susanna's father? What is your evidence?

5. How does Tituba explain the behavior of the girls who meet at the parsonage? Imagine that you are not treated like a child but not considered an adult. Your behavior is severely restricted (remember, bright colors are frippery). Might you seek the company of someone who gave you attention, even if it meant breaking some rules? Explain your answer.

6. Why did Susanna give all the contents of her cart to Sarah Good? Why didn't her mother approve? Who do you think was right—Susanna or her mother? Why?

7. What happened the second time Susanna went to see Tituba? How did these events make her feel? Why did she still want to go back? Under the same circumstances, would you have wanted to go back to the parsonage?

8. Why did William Hobbs come to the English family's home? Can you connect Abigail's behavior to the behavior of the girls at the parsonage? Try to come up with one explanation for both types of behavior.

(for use after reading chapters 7-12)

9. Why didn't Susanna speak out as soon as the girls started making accusations? Given the circumstances, do you think it was a good decision? Given what we now know, do you think it was a good decision? After Susanna's visit to Ann Putnam, would you have changed your mind if you were Susanna? Would your reasoning for not telling have changed?

10. Joseph Putnam says that hysteria feeds on "distrust in our community, on old quarrels between neighbors." Based on what you have read, why did distrust and quarrels exist in Salem? Do you think such distrust and quarrels could feed hysteria in any community, or were there special circumstances in Salem that allowed the hysteria to grow?

11. Describe the scene at which the first three people are accused of being witches. Why does Susanna think those three people were named? What does Susanna hope Tituba will do? What does Tituba actually do? Why? Do you agree with Tituba's thinking?

12. What did Mrs. English do at meeting when the congregation shunned Sarah Cloyce? What do you think the consequences of this action will be?

(for use after reading chapters 13-18)

13. How is the term *break charity* used with respect to Mary Warren? Is this what you thought the phrase meant? Who else in the story could be said to have broken charity? Is breaking charity a good or bad thing to do?

14. Were your predictions about the consequences of Mrs. English's actions correct? How did Susanna react? Why didn't she break charity with the "afflicted girls" after her mother was arrested?

15. Why did Susanna want to stay in Salem when her family went to Boston? Do you think this was a good decision? Explain your answer.

16. What kind of people were Elizabeth and Joseph Putnam? What characteristics did the English girls especially appreciate about the Putnams? Do you think the Putnams were heroes? Why or why not?

17. What was the Court of Oyer and Terminer? How was it established? What evidence did the court look for to determine if an accused person was a witch? Do you think this evidence is valid? Would it be allowed in court today? Why did even a group of ministers think "spectral evidence" should not be considered?

18. Why did Susanna not tell her story, even after the first accused witches were hung? When she finally sits down to tell Joseph, how do you think he will react? How would you react in these circumstances?

(for use after reading chapters 19-23)

19. Were your predictions about Joseph's reactions accurate? Who do you feel more empathy for—Joseph or Susanna?

20. What events combine to cause Susanna to wonder if witchcraft might exist after all? How does Johnathan convince her she is wrong?

21. How do Joseph and his network of people working against witch trials use Susanna's information? Do you think it had an effect? What other factors contributed to Governor Phips's actions?

(for use after reading the epilogue)

22. What was the aftermath of the trials? Why do you think Susanna forgives Ann after all? Do you think Susanna has forgiven herself?

23. Could a witch hunt happen again? Has a witch hunt ever happened again?

Follow-up Activities

1. Read the "Author's Note" with the class and discuss the information it presents. What is the author's explanation for the witch hysteria? What are the strengths of her explanation? What are its weaknesses?

2. Discuss with students what they learned about the Puritans from this book that was new or surprising.

3. Tell students that throughout U.S. history, people have drawn comparisons between other events and the witch trials. For example, the McCarthy hearings regarding alleged Communists in the government were often called a "witch hunt." Arthur Miller even wrote the play The Crucible to make this point. As students read newspapers and magazines, they should look for references to "witch hunts" and bring any such references to class for discussion. Are the analogies made appropriate? Why or why not? Why is this such a powerful phrase?

THEMATIC UNITS, CHILDREN'S LITERATURE, AND HISTORY

Introduction

The three units that follow are intended to serve as models for ways in which works of children's literature can serve as the centerpiece or the stimulant for interdisciplinary units that develop historical understandings. The units are flexible, requiring as few as three class periods to complete but expandable to fill as many as ten. They blend literature/language arts and history with other subject matter and skills.

The first unit, "The American Quilt in Children's Literature," focuses on the quilt as a metaphor for important American values and beliefs. Teachers can select two or more stories from a list of five to help students identify what values the quilt represents. The books listed make the unit suitable for students in grades K-3, although teachers could identify more difficult books to adapt the unit for use with older students.

The second unit, "Bull Run: Examining Historical Perspectives," is based on Paul Fleischman's book, *Bull Run*. This book presents narratives about a single event from the perspectives of 16 different people, allowing students to examine how such factors as race, sex, social class, and place of origin influence an individual's point of view. Suitable for students in grades 4-6, the unit involves a reader's theatre activity, as well as research and writing.

The final unit, "Freedom's Children: An Oral History Unit on the Civil Rights Movement," involves fifth- and sixth-grade students in an examination of racism, prejudice, and the civil rights movement through a collection of oral histories. After they read these moving recollections, they plan and implement an oral history project of their own.

Unit Overview

Quilts are a powerful metaphor in literature, including both contemporary and historical children's literature as well as adult novels. In her book *How to Make an American Quilt* (New York: Villard Books, 1991), Whitney Otto explains part of the image's power when she says "The impulse to unify and separate, rend and join, is powerful and constant." In the quilt, differences are bound together. The quilt is useful beauty, constructed with no waste, and reflecting discipline, organization, and simplicity. Because it is constructed in a social setting and passed from generation to generation, the quilt represents connections among people. As a women's art form, the quilt gives voice to the voiceless. Quilts are also a link to our nation's past, a reminder of what we perceive as a simpler, more self-sufficient time.

While early elementary students are not likely to appreciate all of these aspects of the metaphorical uses of the quilt, they can gain important historical insights through activities revolving around quilts and their use in literature. This unit is flexible, in that it suggests several children's books from which teachers can select one or more books for student reading and discussion.

Historical Understandings: At the end of this unit, students will be able to:

1. Compare and contrast how and why quilts have been made and used by different groups of people and at different times in U.S. history.

2. List some of the reasons quilts are important to people, including important values that quilts represent.

3. Describe an author's purpose in using a quilt as a major story element.

Grade Level: K-3

Time Required: 3-6 class periods depending on the number of stories selected for reading and discussion

Materials and Preparation: If possible, bring several quilts or large color photographs of quilts to class for students to examine. The ideal would be to have one crazy quilt, one patterned quilt, and one pictorial quilt. If neither real quilts or photographs are available, you can use the outlines on Handouts 2-4; these could either be copied for each student or blown up onto sheets of posting paper.

Make copies of Handout 5 for all students. You will also need copies of two or more of these books (arranged from easiest to most difficult):

The Quilt Story, by Tony Johnston, illustrated by Tomie dePaola (New York: Putnam's, 1985).

The Keeping Quilt, by Patricia Polacco (New York: Simon and Schuster, 1988).

The Patchwork Quilt, by Valerie Flournoy, illustrated by Jerry Pinkney (New York: E.P. Dutton, 1985).

Sweet Clara and the Freedom Quilt, by Deborah Hopkinson, illustrated by James Ransome (New York: Alfred Knopf, 1993).

The Canada Geese Quilt, by Natalie Kinsey-Warnock, illustrated by Leslie W. Bowman (New York: Cobblehill Books/Dutton, 1989).

If you plan to have students read and discuss the books in small groups, you will need to make copies of the discussion questions for use in the small groups. It may work best to put the questions on large sheets of posting paper.

Depending on how you plan to end the unit, you may need art or sewing supplies.

Procedure:

1. Display the quilts or quilt pictures you have brought to class. First ask students to list all the things that are the same about the quilts. (Possible answers include they are beautiful, they could keep someone warm, they are made from small pieces of cloth, they are made from layers of material sewn together with something puffy in between.) Post their answers on the chalkboard.

Next, ask students to list all the things that are different about the quilts. (Possible answers include colors, type of pattern, number of pieces of material used, type of material used.) List these answers on the chalkboard as well.

2. Ask students to stand in front of the quilt or picture that they like best. Point out that they have created a human graph; they can tell which quilt is most and least liked by looking at the length of the line of people in front of the quilt. (If you want to follow up on the graphing aspect of the activity, you can tally the number of students favoring each quilt and have students graph the information.) Ask one or two students in each line why they chose that quilt as their favorite. Write their responses in a third list on the chalkboard.

3. Ask students to look at the three lists on the chalkboard and indicate which items listed are reasons that people like quilts. Check these items. What are some other reasons that people like quilts? (Possible answers include they are fun to make, they are presents from older family members, the materials they are made of remind us of family stories, they are both beautiful and useful.)

4. Tell students that people have made quilts for a long time. Depending on the age of the students, distribute Handout 5, or share the information from the handout with students. Allow time for students to discuss the information, drawing their attention to connections between the history of quilting and why people like quilts.

5. Read the poem below to students.

Quilt, by Samantha Abeel*

In the sun, my grandmother would sit,
calico and gingham spread long,
like a river speckled in fall leaves,
over her skirt.
Slowly gathering the pieces,
bringing them together
she would rock, needle in hand.
"Life is a quilt made of many different
faces,"
she used to say,
"a fabric
of different goals and dreams,
each with different colors,
different eyes,
different hands,
yet bound together by a single piece of thread."

Conduct a class discussion of the poem, using the following questions:

- What is the grandmother in the poem doing?

- What does the grandmother compare a quilt to?

- How does the grandmother say the quilt is like life?

- Do you think the comparison is a good one? Why or why not?

6. Tell students that many writers, like Samantha Abeel, use quilts in their writing. Some compare quilts to other things to help us understand their ideas. Other people use quilts in their stories or poems to show what is important to people. In this unit, students are going to read stories that use quilts and try to decide why the writers used quilts. We recommend that you use at least two of the stories to allow for comparisons.

7. Depending on the age of students, you may want to have the reading and discussion done in small groups; all groups can read the same book or each group can read a different book. With younger students, you will likely want to read and discuss each book with the entire class.

The Quilt Story

Mother makes a quilt for Abigail, who uses it for a multitude of purposes—she has tea parties on it, hides under it, wears it, and more. When the family moves West, the quilt goes too, providing Abigail's only link to home. When she gets older, the quilt is put in the attic and forgotten. Animals live in it until another little girl finds it and asks her mother to mend it. When her family moves, she, too, finds comfort in the quilt.

- When do you think Abigail lived? What clues does the story give?

- Why did Abigail's mother make the quilt? Is that the only thing Abigail used the quilt for? Can you think of something you like that you use for many purposes?

- How did Abigail feel about her new home? How did the quilt help her?

_____

"Quilt" is excerpted from *Reach for the Moon*, copyright 1994 Samantha Abeel and Charles R. Murphy. The book is available for $17.95 at local bookstores or direct from Pfeifer-Hamilton Publishers, 210 West Michigan, Duluth, MN 55802, 800-247-6789.

- Why do you think Abigail put the quilt in the attic? Can you think of something you loved but later put away?

- How is the little girl who found the quilt in the attic like Abigail? How is she different? Do you think she will someday put the quilt away?

- How does the author use the quilt to show something he thinks is important to people? Why was the quilt a good way to show this?

The Keeping Quilt

The author's great-grandmother Anna moves from Russia to New York; her only familiar possessions are her dress and babushka. When they are worn out, her mother makes them into a quilt with other discarded family clothing. Throughout the family's history, the quilt serves many functions, eventually being passed down to the author, who plans to give it to her daughter.

- How did Anna feel when she came to New York? How was New York different from Russia? What did she have to remind her of home?

- Whose idea was it to make the quilt? Was it a good idea? Why or why not?

- How was the quilt made? How did Anna help? Do you think the way the quilt was made makes it special, too?

- List some of the ways the quilt was used. How many generations used the quilt? Why do you think members of the family kept using the quilt?

- Do you think the quilt stayed as brightly colored as it is shown in the illustrations? Why do you think Patricia Polacco chose to show the quilt that way?

- How did the author use the quilt to show something she thinks is important to people? Was the quilt a good way to show this? Why or why not?

The Patchwork Quilt

Tanya and her grandma decide to make a quilt from the scraps her grandma has saved from the family's clothing. When Grandma becomes ill, Tanya takes up her grandmother's work, with help from her parents and brothers. She even cuts a square of fabric from her grandmother's old quilt so that Grandma will be in the quilt, too. Finally, Grandma is well enough to finish sewing the quilt, which she gives to Tanya.

- What do Tanya's mother and grandmother say about quilts? What did Grandma mean when she said "sometimes the old ways are forgotten"? Do her daughter's comments about buying a quilt suggest that Grandma is correct?

- How were Jim and Tanya in the quilt? How did it tell their life stories?

- Why does Tanya say Grandma and the quilt are "telling each other stories"? Do you think her mother understands? What evidence can you find to support your answer?

- How do you think Tanya's brothers and parents felt about her working on the quilt? Explain your answer.

- What was wrong with the quilt? What did Tanya do to fix it?

- Imagine that you are Tanya as a grandmother. What will you tell your grandchildren about quilts?

- How does the author use the quilt to show something she thinks is important to people? Was the quilt a good way to show this? Why or why not?

Sweet Clara and the Freedom Quilt

Sweet Clara is taken away from her mother at age 12 to work in the fields at a neighboring plantation. While she longs to return to her mother, kind Aunt Rachel teaches her to sew so she can work in the house instead of the fields. After hearing about the Underground Railroad, Sweet Clara decides to sew a map north on a quilt. When the quilt is finished, she and her friend Jack head north, stopping to pick up her mother and sister on the way. Aunt Rachel keeps the quilt to help other slaves find their way to freedom.

- When did this story take place? What clues can you find in the story?

- Why was Sweet Clara taken from her mother? How did she feel? How does hearing this part of the story make you feel?

- How did Aunt Rachel think learning to sew would help Sweet Clara? Was she right?

- Why did Sweet Clara decide to sew a quilt that showed a map north? How do you think people found out she was making the quilt so they could give her information?

- Why did Sweet Clara say the quilt wouldn't be restful? Do you think she was right?

- What did Sweet Clara mean when she said traveling north was like "being in a dream you already dreamed"? Was the map quilt a dream? Was freedom a dream?

- How did the author use the quilt to show something she thinks is important to people? Was the quilt a good way to show this? Why or why not?

The Canada Geese Quilt

Ariel hates sewing, but she loves drawing and watching her grandmother quilt. When they find out that Ariel's mother is pregnant, Ariel and her grandmother decide to work together on a quilt for the new baby. Ariel creates the design and her grandmother does the sewing. After her grandmother has a stroke, Ariel must take over the quilting. When the baby is born, Ariel learns that her grandmother has made her a special quilt, too.

- When do you think this story took place? What clues do you have?

- What did Grandma do with the quilts she made? How do Mama and Ariel use their artistic talents? How did Grandma and Ariel decide to combine their talents to make a gift for the baby?

- Why do you think April wrapped herself in the iris quilt when her grandmother went to the hospital?

- Why did April start working on the quilt, even though she hated sewing? Did she enjoy making the quilt? How do you think she'll remember this time when she is older?

- How did the picture in the quilt Grandma made for April especially suit her? How do you think receiving this quilt made her feel?

- Imagine that you are Ariel telling your little brother about the time when she and Grandma made the quilt. What would you say? How would you explain the importance of the quilts to your little brother?

- How does the author use the quilt to show something she thinks is important to people? Was the quilt a good way to show this? Why or why not?

8. Following discussion of the individual books, encourage students to make comparisons by asking such questions as:

- What did you notice about who made the quilts in all the stories?

- How were the reasons people made the quilts similar or different?

- What was similar about how people used the quilts? What was different?

- Which quilt did you think was most beautiful? Why?

- Which quilt story did you like best? Why? Did that author use the quilt to show things that you think are important, like freedom, family love, or the specialness of one person?

9. Conclude the unit with an activity in which students, working individually, in small groups, or as a class, create quilt designs. The designs can be either drawn or created in fabric or construction paper, if time permits. The following prompts, based on the various stories, can be used to get students started with their designs. In each case, students should be reminded to design the quilt to show something important to them or something important about quilts.

- Design a quilt that includes your name somewhere in the design.

- Design a quilt using material from two items of clothing that are especially important to you, as well as one item of clothing from two family members or friends.

- Design a map quilt that shows how to get somewhere important.

- Design a quilt that shows what is special about you.

Many classic quilt patterns are reproduced in *A Color Sampler*, by Kathleen Westray (New York: Ticknor and Fields, 1993), a book that deals with the interactions of color and human perception of color. The book would be a useful resource in creating quilt designs.

Another useful resource for design activities is *Eight Hands Round: A Patchwork Alphabet*, by Ann Whitford Paul, illustrated by Jeanette Winter (New York: HarperCollins, 1991). For each letter of the alphabet, this book provides a drawing of a quilt pattern, a close up of one square from the pattern, an explanation of the pattern, and a drawing that more concretely represents that source. For example, for the letter W, the book focuses on the pattern known as Windmill, depicting an actual windmill, describing the use of windmills in the early days of the United States, and showing the windmill pattern and resulting quilt. Considerable historical information is provided in the explanations. Careful study of the illustrations may give students ideas for their own quilt patterns based on everyday things in their environment.

If you decide to have the class work together to actually create a quilt, you may want to share the book, *Huskings, Quiltings, and Barn Raisings: Work-Play Parties in Early America*, by Victoria Wherrow, illustrated by Laura LoTurco (New York: Walker and Co., 1992), with them. It focuses on various kinds of communal work activities that also served as social events in early America. Recipes for foods people ate at these events are provided so that students could prepare and eat similar items during their quilting activities.

A Crazy Quilt

A Quilt Made from a Pattern

A Picture Quilt

The Story of Quilts

Quilts have been made for thousands of years. A quilt has three layers. The top layer is usually made of small pieces of fabric sewn together. (Sometimes the top layer is made of one large piece of fabric with a pattern sewn in with thread.) The bottom layer is made of one large piece of fabric. The middle layer is a layer of padding. The layers are stitched together or tied through.

In early America, people made quilts to stay warm. They used patchwork because it was often hard to get fabric. The plain fabric used for the back was often made at home, too.

A woman would sew patches from worn-out clothing into squares or other pieces. These pieces would then be sewn together into the quilt top. The layers of the quilt would often be sewn together at a quilting bee—a gathering where several women sat around a frame, quilting. During long, lonely winters, quilting bees provided a break. Quilting bees would go on all day. Girls too young to quilt would thread needles or make rag rugs while the women sewed.

The men would arrive in time for supper. Sometimes there would be dancing or games after supper. One game was tossing children in the air on the new quilts. This game was fun and showed how strong the quilts were.

Often, a quilt was the only patch of color in a dreary cabin. By making quilts, women not only made something useful for their families. They also created something of lasting beauty.

American quilters created many quilt patterns. A pattern might be based on nature, family stories, everyday items, or the Bible. Other quilters preferred the crazy quilt, in which the pieces do not form a pattern. Still other quilters created picture quilts or quilts that tell stories.

When people moved away from a community, their neighbors sometimes made friendship quilts. Each person made a square that showed something special to them. That person's name was stitched on the square. The squares were then made into a quilt and given to the departing friend.

Quilts have added beauty to American homes for many years. They have also had many different uses. Today, quilts that have been passed down through families are a way to learn about history, too.

Bull Run: Examining Historical Perspectives

Unit Overview

Bull Run, by Paul Fleischman, illustrated by David Frampton (New York: Harper Collins, 1993), presents narratives from 16 people—half with Northern perspectives and half with Southern—on events leading up to and during the first battle at Bull Run. Through the eyes of such people as a Minnesota girl whose brother runs away to fight, a slave woman who accompanies her owner to battle, the driver of a hired carriage who drives congressmen and their wives to picnic as they watch the battle, military leaders on both sides, a German immigrant fighting for the North, and an adolescent Georgia boy eager to take part in a battle, the reader gains a unique perspective on this Civil War battle and on how historical events are perceived differently by different people.

The author suggests presenting the book through a readers' theatre approach, an approach that we have integrated into this unit. The unit would be most appropriately used when students are studying the Civil War, since some understanding of that conflict will provide a broader context for discussion of the novel and the battle that it describes.

Historical Understandings: At the end of this unit, students will be able to:

1. Recognize that different individuals have different perspectives on the same historic events.

2. Explain some of the factors (race, gender, age, region lived in, religion) that influence an individual's perspective on a historic event.

3. Identify ways in which personal decisions interact with other causes to shape events.

4. Analyze the process by which a textbook writer or historian distills extensive information and numerous perspectives into a brief account.

5. Identify perspectives that are missing from textbook accounts of historic events.

Grade Level: 4-6

Time Required: 5 class periods

Materials and Preparation: You will need several copies of the book *Bull Run*. For the readers' theater portion of the lesson, you may want to copy one or two sets of each character's pages, as well as Handout 6. You will also need copies of Handout 7, as well as other resource materials on the Civil War. The librarian/media specialist may be able to help you locate a variety of resources, including books, appropriate articles from such magazines as *American Heritage*, PBS videos, and photographs.

Procedure

1. Begin the unit by asking students to take about ten minutes to describe something about their experiences of the day. They should focus on something that occurred at school. Their accounts should include information about what occurred, as well as their thoughts about the event(s). Some students will be asked to share their accounts with the class, so they should not write about anything that is too private to be shared.

2. After ten minutes have elapsed, ask four or five students to share what they have written. Following the reading of these accounts, ask students to comment on whether a coherent history of this day at school emerges from the accounts. Why or why not? Do they think the different accounts and reactions would be typical of how people perceive all events?

3. Next, give students Handout 6 or read aloud its account of the Battle of Bull Run. This description is typical of textbook accounts of the event. Does this account help readers understand the different ways in which people experienced the battle? Why or why not?

4. Tell students that they are going to be reading a book that will help them understand the different ways in which the Battle of Bull Run was experienced by different people. They will be reading the book in a readers' theatre format. If students have not previously taken part in readers' theatre activities, explain that readers' theatre is a method of shared oral reading. The book students are going to read is told through the voices of 16 characters, for whom students will be providing the voices.

5. Assign roles to students. Depending on the size of your class, some roles may have only one student, while others have two. Pass out copies of the appropriate pages to students, along with Handout 7, and explain how the reading will occur.

6. Allow time for students to read through the passages that they will read aloud. You may want to have students create large copies of the woodcuts for their characters, along with the name of the character and where he/she was from, on posterboard. These poster-boards can then be displayed while a character is speaking/reading; in cases where two students split a role, these visuals could be helpful in identifying who is speaking.

7. Conduct the reading of the book, which will probably take two class periods. At the end of the first class period, you may want to allow time for students to reflect on what they have heard so far, either through discussion or a brief writing activity. The reflection could be focused on one of the following questions, or another open-ended question of your choosing:

   - How are the different characters' views of war similar or different?

   - What do Northerners think about Southerners? What do Southerners think about Northerners?

   - Whose perspective do you find it easiest to understand or empathize with so far? Why? Whose perspective is hardest for you to understand?

8. When students have completed the book, conduct a class discussion, using such questions as those given in step 7 above or the following:

   - Which of the characters in the story do you think were courageous? Would you call any of the characters heroes? Why or why not?

- Pick a character from the story. What decision did this person make that influenced his/her experience of the battle? What decisions made by someone else influenced this person?

- How do the different perspectives in the book help you better understand what happened at Bull Run? How would you explain some of the contradictions in the accounts from different people?

- What factors do you think were most important in determining a person's perspective on the war—age, race, gender, where the person was from, religion?

- What do you think the author's view of the Civil War is? What evidence can you give to support your answer?

9. Tell students that they are going to revise the textbook account on Handout 6 to give a richer understanding of what happened at Bull Run. In order to do that, they need to do some additional research about the battle. Divide the class into small groups of three to four students. Each group should conduct its own research on the battle of Bull Run. Students may find it useful to begin by using what they have learned from the book to create a map and accompanying timeline of troop movements and events leading up to the battle and during the battle. They can then revise these tools to reflect new information as they gather it. Each group should use at least two additional sources besides the textbook account and *Bull Run*. Allow at least one class period for the research.

10. When students have completed their research, direct them to synthesize what they have learned into a 250-word account of the battle, which can be accompanied by one illustration. When the groups have completed their work, have two groups work together to share and compare their accounts. How similar are the two accounts? How did the thinking processes of the two groups result in different accounts?

11. Conclude the unit with a class discussion of the challenges that historians and textbook writers face when they must distill a great deal of information into a brief description. How did this experience help students understand the work of a historian? How did it help them learn to evaluate information in a history textbook more skillfully?

Note to Teachers: You might return to the concept of multiple perspectives throughout your study of the Civil War, having students research another event (e.g., Lee's surrender at Appomattox, Lincoln's assassination) and then write about the event from the perspective of different characters. As an alternative, each student could create a character to "become" during study of the Civil War, keeping a civil war diary from that character's perspective. Students could share their diaries to see how events affected different people differently.

The Battle of Bull Run: A Textbook Description

Fort Sumter fell in April 1861, starting the Civil War. Most Americans believed the war would be short. Many thought that one huge battle would decide the war. With the Confederate capital of Richmond only 100 miles from Washington, DC, it seemed certain that a major battle would occur between the two cities during the summer of 1861.

Confederate forces—approximately 21,000 men under the command of General P.G.T. Beauregard—were in position at Manassas Junction, Virginia. Manassas was an important railroad center. A smaller group under the leadership of General Joseph Johnston guarded Harpers Ferry.

General Irvin McDowell of the Union Army was in Washington, trying to mold thousands of new volunteers into an army. General Robert Patterson of the Union Army was threatening Harpers Ferry in Virginia. Although Union army leaders argued that their forces were not ready for battle, politicians, the press, and the public pressured General McDowell to begin an advance. Under orders, McDowell began his advance in July with 39,000 men.

The march of the Union army from Washington to Manassas was very slow due to lack of discipline among the soldiers and extreme heat. When McDowell paused to rest his troops and devise a plan of attack, General Beauregard gathered his scattered forces. General Johnston's troops were able to travel from Harper's Ferry to Manassas, something the Union forces did not know.

The battle that followed was fought on July 21, at a stream called Bull Run. While the Union troops were initially successful in pushing back the Confederates, fresh troops led a Confederate counterattack. The Union troops fell into disarray, retreating wildly towards Washington. Although the Confederate troops pursued the Union forces toward Centreville, they were too tired and disorganized to follow the Union troops back to Washington. If they had, the South might have won the war then and there. Instead, the long war was on.

Conducting a Reader's Theatre Activity Using Paul Fleischman's *Bull Run*

Reader's Theatre is a shared oral reading. The 16 characters in the book *Bull Run* will each be read by different people. Your teacher will assign you—and perhaps a partner—to be one character. It may be helpful to the class to prepare a sign with your character's name. You may want to decorate the sign with the woodcut illustration beneath your character's name in the book or with some other artwork that represents your character.

To help you identify when it is your turn to read, the list belows shows the order of the parts.

1. Colonel Oliver Brattle
2. Lily Malloy
3. Shem Suggs
4. Gideon Adams
5. Flora Wheelworth
6. James Dacy
7. Toby Boyce
8. Gideon Adams
9. Virgil Peavey
10. Nathaniel Epp
11. Shem Suggs
12. Dietrich Herz
13. Dr. William Rye
14. Lily Malloy
15. Toby Boyce
16. James Dacy
17. Judah Jenkins
18. General Irvin McDowell
19. Flora Wheelworth
20. Gideon Adams
21. Colonel Oliver Brattle
22. A.B. Tilbury
23. Carlotta King
24. Nathaniel Epp
25. Virgil Peavey
26. General Irvin McDowell
27. Shem Suggs
28. Gideon Adams
29. Flora Wheelworth
30. Edmund Upwing
31. Judah Jenkins
32. Dietrich Herz
33. Toby Boyce
34. James Dacy
35. Colonel Oliver Brattle
36. A.B. Tilbury
37. Dr. William Rye
38. Edmund Upwing
39. Virgil Peavey
40. Dietrich Herz
41. Carlotta King
42. Gideon Adams
43. Judah Jenkins
44. A.B. Tilbury
45. Shem Suggs
46. General Irvin McDowell
47. Toby Boyce
48. James Dacy
49. Colonel Oliver Brattle
50. Edmund Upwing
51. Carlotta King
52. Dietrich Herz
53. Shem Suggs
54. Nathaniel Epp
55. Dr. William Rye
56. Gideon Adams
57. Toby Boyce
58. Edmund Upwing
59. Flora Wheelworth
60. Lily Malloy

Unit Overview

Today's young people often do not believe that people their age can make a difference. Nor do they understand our country's legacy related to race relations; they do not realize the cruel extent or institutionalized nature of racism and discrimination that existed only decades ago, nor do they appreciate the courage and determination of the Americans of all races who risked everything to end racism and discrimination. In *Freedom's Children: Young Civil Rights Activists Tell Their Own Stories* (New York: Avon, 1994 [paperback]), editor Ellen Levine presents powerful excerpts from interviews with 30 African Americans who were active as young people in the civil rights movement of the 1950s and 1960s. These stories provide a window into both the positive and negative legacies and stand as evidence that young people can make a difference.

The first half of this two-part unit involves students in reading and discussing sections of Levine's collection of oral histories. The second half of the unit challenges them to conduct their own oral histories, focusing on young people's contributions either to the civil rights movement or to another effort for social change with particular relevance to your community.

Historical Understandings: At the end of this unit, students will be able to:

1. Describe the racism and prejudice faced by African Americans at the middle of the 20th century.

2. Recognize that individuals, including young people, can help bring about social change.

3. Explain reasons and personal qualities that led people to become involved in efforts for social change.

4. Evaluate oral history information in terms of its reliability.

5. Gather information through oral history interviews and analyze that information in light of other available facts/generalizations.

Grade Level: 5-6

Time Required: 5-10 or more class periods depending on the scope of the oral history activity you decide to undertake with the class

Materials and Preparation: Because of the complexity of this unit, the materials you will need and preparation to be undertaken are broken into two parts—those needed for reading and discussion of the book and those needed for conducting an oral history project with students.

Part 1: You will need a selection of newspapers saved over several days or weeks before you begin teaching the unit; you may want to ask students and/or other teachers to help you collect papers. You will also need at least seven copies of the book *Freedom's Children*, copies of Handout 8 for all students, and seven colors of marker.

Prior to beginning the lesson, make a large timeline on shelf paper. On the timeline, include the years from 1950 to 1970 (students can later expand the timeline if they wish to); put a few of the major events from the chronology at the end of *Freedom's Children* on the timeline, but leave most of it blank so students can add information as they work on the unit.

Part 2: You will need copies of Handout 9 for all students. You will also need several portable tape recorders and tapes. Before you begin the lesson, spend some time thinking about a focus for the oral history project students are to conduct; if possible, focus on the role of young people in the civil rights movement. If this is not possible in your community, choose a similar focus: that is, try to focus on the role of young people in working for social change. In your particular community, a focus such as the rights of migrant farm workers, environmental issues, the Equal Rights Amendment, or the 18-year-old voting rights issue may be more appropriate.

When you have selected your focus, arrange for several community members to visit your class and be interviewed by students (having interviewees come to students instead of vice versa will pose fewer logistical problems for upper elementary students). Calls to churches, community groups, and other organizations can be a useful way to begin locating potential interviewees. Students' parents or grandparents may also be possibilities. As Levine describes in the introduction to her book, finding one person can often lead to others. If possible, obtain some basic biographical information on each person and prepare an index card for each person with their name, age, and other basic data. You may want to encourage the interview subjects to bring pictures, other visuals, or artifacts with them on the day the interviews are to take place.

On the day the interviews are to be conducted, you may need to make arrangements for additional space for the class, so that several interviews can be conducted simultaneously without interfering with one another. If you want to expand your project to allow publication of the oral histories students collect, you may need to arrange for computer time and/or assistance from a parent or aide who can help with typing and production.

Procedure

Part 1

1. Write the following statement on the chalkboard:

Young people can help make our world a better place to live.

Ask students whether they agree or disagree with this statement. Write the tally of their responses on the chalkboard. Ask one or two students on each side of the issue to explain the reasons for their position.

© 1995 Social Science Education Consortium

2. Next, tell the students you want them to look for evidence to support the chalkboard statement in the newspapers you have gathered. You may want to provide an example of an article you have found that tells about young people performing service, raising funds for a worthy cause, or taking part in a protest; write a "headline" summarizing your example (e.g., Students Meet to Discuss Violence in Schools) on the chalkboard near the original statement. Have the students work in pairs or triads to look for evidence to support the statement. Each pair or triad should create a headline for each piece of evidence they find; have them write their headlines on the chalkboard around the original statement, just as you did for the example.

3. Tell students that they are going to be reading a book about a time when many young—and old—people worked hard to make our country a better place. Read the following excerpt from the book to students:

> Going to jail, oh, it was a badge of honor during that time! When you demonstrated, you already knew it's possible you're going to jail. It's possible you're gonna get hurt. It's possible you're gonna get killed. But our minds were made up...We just had our minds set on freedom, and that was it—Gladis Williams

Ask students to speculate on what time Ms. Williams is talking about. Accept all answers.

4. Share with students the title of the book, making sure they understand the term "civil rights activists." Explain that the book is a collection of oral histories—descriptions of events gathered through interviews with people directly involved in those events. Read the book's "Introduction" aloud and discuss it with the class, making sure they have some general understanding of the civil rights movement and the problems it was aimed at solving.

5. Divide the class into seven groups of students, assigning each group one of the chapters of the book. Each group should read its chapter and use the questions on Handout 8 to discuss what they have read. Give each group a different colored marker so they can add events mentioned in their chapter to the timeline. Allow at least one class period for the reading and discussion.

6. When groups have completed their discussion, they should plan a five- to seven-minute presentation that will inform their classmates of some of the most important ideas that emerged from the chapter and their discussion. Encourage students to be creative in planning their presentations, which could be in such formats as a choral reading, a dramatization of an event described in the chapter, or a simulated press conference. The planning and presentation stages will each require one class period to complete.

7. Following the presentations, conduct a discussion of the book with students, focusing both on the substance of the book and the use of oral histories as a source. The following questions may be useful in stimulating discussion:

- Were there examples of racism and discrimination that surprised you? What were they? What about these examples surprised you? (e.g., the severity, the fact that such discrimination was legal) Could this kind of racism or discrimination occur today? Why or why not?

- What motivated the young people in the book to become involved in the civil rights movement? Do you think they shared any special characteristics? If so, what were they? Ellen Levine called the people she interviewed "Freedom's Children." Can you think of a better name for the book?

- What reasons for not participating in the civil rights movement were mentioned in the book? Do you think these reasons were valid? Why or why not?

- Do you think the civil rights movement was successful? How would you define *success* in this case?

- Did you find any disagreements about facts or events in the oral history stories? If so, what do you think accounts for those disagreements? How could you check the accuracy of the two conflicting statements?

- What other kinds of sources do you think you would need to read to become an "expert" on the civil rights movement? What would those sources have that the oral histories do not have? What do the oral histories have that other sources might not?

- What questions do you think Ellen Levine asked to get the stories presented in her book? What questions would you like to ask someone who participated in the civil rights movement if you had a chance to talk with such a person?

Part 2

8. Tell students that they are going to be conducting an oral history project of their own, focusing on young people's role in the civil rights movement in your community (or on another topic you have selected because of its relevance to your community). People who were involved in this effort as young people will be visiting your class in a few days to be interviewed.

9. Distribute Handout 9 and go over it with students. In small groups or as a class, have students develop a list of questions for use in their interviews. If students work in small groups, collect the questions from all the groups and have the class as a whole decide which questions will be asked. If time permits, you may want to role play a portion of an interview so that students get the idea of asking follow-up questions.

10. Divide the class into as many small groups as you have people lined up to be interviewed. Give each group the name of the person they will interview, along with any background information that you have. Have each group decide on a strategy for asking the questions. For this age, it may work best to have each question assigned to one student. Groups may need a chance to practice using the tape recorder.

11. On the day the interviews are to be conducted, make sure that all the groups have enough space to conduct their interviews without interfering with other groups. Each group will also need a functioning tape recorder and tape. Circulate among the groups to trouble shoot as needed.

12. On the day following the interviews, allow time for groups to write thank you notes to their interviewees. Conduct a brief discussion of how the students generally felt the interviews went, using such questions as the following to prompt discussion:

- What questions were effective in generating relevant responses?

- What questions were less effective?

- Was it hard to keep the interviewee on the topic? What strategies worked to pull the person back to the focus of the interview?

- What good follow-up questions were asked?

- What could students have done to make the interview more productive?

- Did anything happen in your interview to make you question the accuracy of the information the person provided? (e.g., the person giving contradictory information or saying they didn't remember something very well) Did the person you interviewed have a clear point of view or opinion that might influence the way he/she remembered events?

13. Next, have students return to their groups to listen to the tapes or go over their notes, selecting excerpts from their interviews that they think provide the most direct answers to questions the class developed. Have students transcribe these excerpts. If time is limited, you may want to focus on only a few of the questions. Conversely, with more time, you may want to have the tapes transcribed by students, parents, or aides; groups can then prepare more complete answers to the class questions and analyze additional information that emerged unrelated to the questions. If your class project related to the civil rights movement, students may want to add additional information to the timeline.

14. Make the results of all the groups' work available to the class. Allow time for students to read the various accounts and to compare them with information on the same topic found in textbooks, encyclopedias, magazines, and other sources. Are there contradictions? Can the contradictions be resolved? Again, if time permits, students could prepare an exhibit or book based on their interviews and research.

15. To conclude the unit, ask each student to choose one of the following questions and write a one-page essay expressing their views:

- Can young people help make our world a better place to live? Give examples to support your views. Has this unit changed your thinking about what young people can accomplish? Why or why not?

- What motivates people to work for social change? How do you think people who become involved in efforts like the civil rights movement are different from people who do not? Give examples.

- Why do you think oral history is a useful tool in understanding the past? What are oral history's strengths? What are its limitations?

Discussion Questions for *Freedom's Children*

1. What examples of racism are evident in your chapter? What examples of discrimination did you note? Was the discrimination legal or illegal? What was particularly interesting to you about the descriptions of racism and discrimination?

2. What actions did people quoted in the chapter take to end racism and discrimination? How effective do you think these actions were?

3. Why did the people quoted in your chapter become involved in the civil rights movement? List the reasons they give as well as any personal qualities that you can infer from their words. What reasons for not participating are mentioned? Which reasons for either participating or not participating seem most convincing to you?

4. Pick a quotation from your chapter that you find especially interesting. Share your ideas about the quotation with your group and see if they have different views.

5. What person quoted or talked about in the chapter do you find most interesting? Why?

6. If you had been a young person living in the 1950s and 1960s, do you think you would have become involved in the civil rights movement? Why or why not?

Guidelines for Doing Oral History

Oral history is a way to gather information from people who took part in certain past events. Oral history involves interviewing those people and recording their answers. The person being interviewed is often called the interview subject.

Before you conduct an interview, you should plan the questions you want to ask. What information do you want to get? What questions will help you get that information? Write your questions so that they require more than a Yes or No answer. For example, the second question below will get better results than the first:

- Did you take part in the civil rights movement?

- Tell me about the first time you became involved in a civil rights demonstration.

Before you conduct your interview, make sure your tape recorder is working. Label the tape with the date, name, and topic of your interview. You may also want to have a notepad with you so you can write ideas for follow-up questions as the person is talking.

Ask your interview subject if you can tape the conversation. Have them sign a release form like the one on the next page so you can share the information you collect with others.

Begin the interview by asking where and when the interview subject was born. This information will save you from asking several other questions about dates.

If your subject strays from the topic, try to bring them back by asking one of your prepared questions.

Listen carefully while your subject is talking. Often, what a person says may suggest a follow-up question that will produce interesting information. For example, imagine that you asked your subject how his/her parents felt about their child taking part in demonstrations. In answering, the subject mentions that his/her parents were influenced by their minister. You might want to follow up by asking about the minister—what his/her views on the civil rights movement were, why the minister influenced his/her parents, and so on.

Be polite. Provide time for the person to answer questions. Don't argue or correct the subject. Oral histories are not always accurate. But they do provide important information about feelings and impressions.

End by thanking your subject. Follow up with a thank you letter.

Sample Interview Agreement Form

In view of the historical value of this oral history interview, I _____

_____ knowingly and voluntarily permit _____

the full use of this information for educational purposes.

Name_____ Date_____

INDEX OF BOOK TITLES